"*The Unicorn Protocol* offers a welcome departure from the typical startup narrative. Rather than glorifying disruption or relying on post-hoc success stories, it brings forward the operational, emotional, and structural realities of building a company in one of the most unforgiving sectors: healthcare.

This collection of founder stories helps reframe how we evaluate early-stage digital health ventures. It puts founders rather than technologies at the center of the story. In doing so, it surfaces key patterns that matter most, such as how conviction is tested by reimbursement cycles, how clinical validation collides with commercial runway, and how teams evolve under regulatory and cultural pressure.

What makes this book valuable isn't just the access to high-profile founders or the sector-specific anecdotes. It's the cumulative picture it paints of what's required to create momentum in a system that rarely rewards speed or novelty. For the investors, health system partners, and even incumbents in the system, the book offers a more informed lens on what early-stage success actually looks like before scale.

The Unicorn Protocol isn't a hero's journey but rather a map of the terrain, drawn by those who've crossed it."

Ali Tafreshi
CEO and President, Topcon Health, Inc.

"*The Unicorn Protocol* is a refreshingly candid and deeply human exploration of what it takes to build a successful digital health startup. Far from a conventional how-to manual, this founder-centric anthology offers an unfiltered look into the personal journeys of entrepreneurs who have dared to challenge the healthcare status quo. Through rich storytelling, detailed company profiles, and insightful interviews, the book reveals the grit, strategy, and soul behind some of the most impactful healthcare innovations of our time. It doesn't romanticize the startup path – it respects it, honoring the complexity and purpose that drive mission-led founders. For healthcare professionals contemplating entrepreneurship, startup teams navigating early growth, or investors seeking to understand what makes a digital health venture thrive, *The Unicorn Protocol* serves as a compass, a mirror, and a call to action."

Kathleen McGrow *DNP, MS, RN, PMP, FHIMSS, FAAN*
Global Chief Nursing Innovation Officer, Microsoft
Author, Empowering Nurses with Technology: A Practical Guide to Nurse Informatics

"After reading *The Unicorn Protocol* and have to say – I love it. The case study format and founder interviews are just what the 'doctor' ordered. The diversity of experiences and voices brings a richness that makes this a compelling read and a powerful guide for anyone navigating the digital health space.

Many moments stuck with me, and this kind of real-world learning (and listening) sets this book apart. Sally has captured more than the ambition of these founders, but the messy, essential work of earning trust, evolving strategy, and delivering measurable impact. I've watched and met many of these leaders, but reading their retrospective insights – how decisions played out over time – was addictive. *The Unicorn Protocol* has the potential to join the key guides for serial entrepreneurs, first-time founders, and even VCs looking to better understand what makes or breaks a company in the health sector. It should be a required B-school text.

In short, Sally Ann Frank delivers a refreshingly candid guide for digital health founders committed to leading with innovation and heart. Through real-world stories of startup successes and setbacks, she reveals what it truly takes to build scalable, mission-driven companies in a fragmented and high-stakes industry. This isn't a book about hi-tech hype; it's a roadmap for meaningful progress, reminding us that fundamental health transformation starts with purpose and must be driven by impact."

Gil Bashe
Managing Partner, Chair Global Health and Purpose, FINN Partners

"This is a terrific book, yet again!!

I found the anecdotes super informative and insightful. To hear directly from some of the most successful healthcare technology entrepreneurs is powerful. Every entrepreneur and investor innovating in healthcare will be better learning what these leaders did right and wrong."

Michael A. Greeley
General Partner, Flare Capital Partners

"*The Unicorn Protocol* is an extraordinary guide for anyone serious about building the future of healthcare. Sally Ann Frank brings to life the origin stories of digital health founders who dared to dream big and deliver bigger, often motivated by personal experiences that exposed the system's failures.

Unlike other books filled with buzzwords or bravado, this book is about real founders solving real problems."

Tom Lawry
Author of Hacking Healthcare *and* Health Care Nation

"*The Unicorn Protocol* is a compelling roadmap for digital health entrepreneurs, offering firsthand insights from founders who've achieved what many only dream of – Unicorn status. Through deeply personal stories, tactical lessons, and candid reflections, Sally Ann Frank captures the grit, missteps, and vision that drive meaningful innovation in healthcare from ten different Unicorn founders. Whether you're building your first MVP or navigating scale, this book delivers invaluable wisdom straight from those who've been there – and made it. I would strongly recommend reading Sally's first book, *The Startup Protocol* ahead of embarking on this one for a completely immersive experience in the world of healthcare startups."

Aly H. Abayazeed, *MD, MS, CIIP*
Neuroradiologist and Founder of QRadAI

"There's immense opportunity in disrupting healthcare with AI – but building and scaling companies in digital health comes with unique, often underestimated challenges.

Even as AI tools evolve rapidly, the principles shared by these founders are invaluable. These interviews are so honest, thorough, and helpful for others wanting to follow this journey. *The Unicorn Protocol* is a concise, practical guidebook that's both inspiring and actionable for anyone building in this space. A must-read for digital health entrepreneurs."

Heena Purohit
Director of AI Startups, Microsoft for Startups, Microsoft

"This book is a must read for anyone building in health tech. Sally does a masterful job of compiling and communicating the stories of the unicorn companies we've all heard of in a truly enjoyable fashion.

The biggest take away from me was how many different paths to success were taken across the various companies. I also found it fascinating to learn about how each company's journey evolved, often ending with a completely different product they thought they had when starting out.

If you are a health tech founder, you will not find another book written with this level of advice and inspiration.

This is truly a niche book that feels like it was written just for me; we all owe Sally a debt of gratitude for putting this together.

(True to Sally's style, no AI was used in the writing of this review or the reading of the book 😂)"

Mendel Erlenwein
Founder and CEO, CareCo

"This is a masterful tapestry of founders' journeys, capturing their raw realities and hard-won breakthroughs. But it's much more than a collection of unicorn success stories. What sets it apart is the author's rare ability to distill patterns, lessons, and defining moments in each founder's path. Her reflections, rooted in deep personal experience with startups, lend a clarity and credibility which complement the book's inspiration. A must-read for anyone serious about understanding what it really takes to create a successful company."

Ranya Habash, *MD*
Bascom Palmer/University of Miami and Founder, Sweet Medical

"Great founders look to the past to help shape the future. Sally shares compelling, real-world stories from the people behind some of today's top healthcare and life science companies, providing a blueprint for the next generation of entrepreneurs."

Elliott Parker
CEO, Alloy Partners

The Unicorn Protocol

As a follow-up to the author's first book, *The Startup Protocol: A Guide for Digital Health Startups to Bypass Pitfalls and Adopt Strategies That Work*, this book is a series of case studies about digital health Unicorns. The ultimate goal is to further educate digital health startup founders and their teams about what it takes to be successful and have a lasting, positive effect on our healthcare delivery system. Through a series of interviews with Unicorn founders and leaders, the book will synthesize the information and highlight the elements that led to the growth and success of the companies.

Building on the template of Ideate, Build, Launch, and Grow outlined in *The Startup Protocol*, this book documents the origin story of each Unicorn and then follows it through the process of building their solution, launching the solution, and growing their company to Unicorn status.

The Unicorn Protocol

Digital Health Unicorns, How They Got There and What You Can Learn from Them

Sally Ann Frank

Foreword by
Stephen Ibaraki, Investor, Futurist, Global Advisor, and Mentor

Routledge
Taylor & Francis Group
A PRODUCTIVITY PRESS BOOK

Designed cover image: Shutterstock

First published 2026
by Routledge
605 Third Avenue, New York, NY 10158

and by Routledge
4 Park Square, Milton Park, Abingdon, Oxon, OX14 4RN

Routledge is an imprint of the Taylor & Francis Group, an informa business

ISBN: 978-1-032-71106-5 (hbk)
ISBN: 978-1-032-71101-0 (pbk)
ISBN: 978-1-032-71103-4 (ebk)

DOI: 10.4324/9781032711034

Typeset in Garamond
by Apex CoVantage, LLC

This book is dedicated to big thinkers and innovative builders. May this book inspire you and enable you to improve everyone's health and wellbeing.

Contents

Preface

As I was finishing *The Startup Protocol*, I realized that the story was incomplete. Helping early-stage founders understand some of the common blind spots and recommendations for overcoming them is just the beginning of what a digital health startup founder needs. I believe most startup founders, especially in healthcare, aspire to positively affect people's lives. They are individuals who are inspired to take action.

Understanding the journey of successful digital health founders, especially those who have achieved Unicorn status, is inspiring to the cohort of startups just beginning their journey and maybe even to those who are further along. There is no single path to building a successful company, but the idea behind this book is that there are valuable lessons to be learned from those who have come before you. We can learn what not to do from defunct startups like Olive, Babylon Health, and the infamous Theranos. But in this book, we will examine some of the top digital health companies to learn what they did right, in hopes that we can learn from their success and the occasional misstep.

It is my hope and theirs that, as you read these pages, you will find strategies, tactics, and inspiration to point you toward success and even Unicorn status.

P.S. This is the work of humans – lots of them. AI tools, in this case Copilot, were only used in the introductions to each chapter for the TLDR (Too Long Didn't Read) section. This book is the product of a painstakingly, detailed review of each interview video and transcript, writing, editing, and confirming that each sentence is consistent with the intent of the founder. Since AI-generated content is all the rage right now, it's important to me that you know, dear reader, that this was crafted by *actual* humans.

Foreword

I first met Sally Ann Frank at a bustling startup private showcase in Detroit. Founders were pitching, but one mentor guided the process, calmly guiding clinicians-innovator-turned-entrepreneurs through their stories until they sparkled. In that instant, I understood something essential about Sally: she doesn't merely cheer from the sidelines – she rolls up her sleeves, clarifies the vision, and propels innovators forward. As an investor, futurist, and long-time advisor within multiple global communities such as IEEE Entrepreneurship, WITSA, Microsoft for Startups, AI for Good Innovation Factory, WFP Innovation Accelerator, CEO-infused organizations, and Sovereign funding, I have witnessed many champions of entrepreneurship; few match Sally's gift for turning bold ideas into healthcare breakthroughs.

That gift radiates through *The Unicorn Protocol.*

Drawing on countless hours spent with founders who steered their digital health companies from "garage" to *Unicorn status* – a feat detailed through candid interviews within these pages – Sally distills what truly separates lasting success from well-intentioned collapse. Building upon The Startup Protocol, she organizes the journey into the stages every venture must navigate – *Ideate, Build, Launch, Grow* – and enriches each phase with candid accounts from leaders from a curated selection of digital health Unicorns like Aidoc, DispatchHealth, Omada Health, and others, detailed within. The result is not another glossy collection of platitudes; it is a *compass* readers can carry into the stormy, exhilarating waters of digital health innovation.

Why This Book Matters Now

Healthcare entrepreneurship isn't for the faint-hearted. Founders must master complex regulations, convince skeptical clinicians, secure rigorous evidence, and still build scalable technology. Even seasoned executives falter under that weight. *The Unicorn Protocol* tackles these realities head-on. You will learn:

- **Resilience with purpose** – how Unicorn founders rebounded from clinical-trial surprises, shifting reimbursement models, and near-fatal cash shortages without losing sight of patient impact.
- **Customer insight beyond surveys** – why the best ideas emerge in hospital corridors and patient homes, not boardrooms, and how listening deeply can *spark crucial product shifts* that redefine a venture's trajectory.
- **Empathy-driven missions** – stories that prove compassion is not a soft metric; it is the engine that attracts talent, investors, and early-adopter clinicians.
- **Prudent, disciplined scaling** – examples of companies that resisted reckless growth, chose focus over flash, and ultimately unlocked far greater value.

As I read these chapters, I found myself underlining passages and scribbling notes – even after decades of leading innovations in technology. That is the mark of a true field guide: it teaches newcomers while still surprising veterans.

A Peer's Perspective

My vantage point is that of an external advisor, mentor, and investor across multiple global startup entities, and I see from an external vantage point the Health and Life Sciences cohort at Microsoft for Startups, where I mentor startups and where Sally leads globally. I see founders arrive each week with extraordinary prototypes and equally daunting blind spots. Many need precisely the roadmap this book provides – one that balances vision with disciplined execution, heart with data, and speed with regulatory respect. Sally's counsel has helped startups secure clinical pilots, land crucial funding, and – yes – achieve billion-dollar valuations. Her lessons are hard-won and time-tested; here, they are yours to apply.

How to Read This Book

Think of each chapter, structured around the critical Ideate, Build, Launch, and Grow phases, as a *conversation with a mentor* who has already charted the labyrinth. Don't rush. Pause after the reflection questions. Compare the founders' setbacks to your own. Better yet, discuss the insights with your team; culture is forged in dialogue, not silence. And when you hit a rough patch – and you will – return to the margins you filled with notes. They will steady your hand.

The Enduring Mission: Beyond the Unicorn Milestone

The lessons of *The Unicorn Protocol* also resonate on a personal level, pointing toward the enduring impact of mission-driven entrepreneurship. While the book masterfully charts the course to Unicorn status for individual startups, the principles of purpose, perseverance, and patient-centricity it champions are vital for long-term success in the broader healthcare ecosystem. I think of innovators like Dr. Stephen Shaya, whose commitment to nurturing multiple businesses (Akkad Holdings, J&B Medical, and over 20 others, including the latest Shamekh IV Solutions) with a steadfast focus on quality and service showcases this ethos. Such careers serve as beacons, illustrating the kind of sustained, mission-centric impact *The Unicorn Protocol* prepares its readers to aspire to, even as they navigate the unique path of their own ventures.

Looking Ahead

The next decade will see diagnostics powered by multimodal AI, hospital-at-home platforms scaling worldwide, and biology rewritten by quantum computing. The entrepreneurs who thrive in that landscape will be the ones who blend *audacity with humility*, exactly as Sally prescribes here. If you are holding this book, you have already signaled your intent to join them.

So, turn the page with confidence. Let these stories remind you that setbacks are classrooms, that breakthroughs often hide inside feedback you dread, and that the most sustainable growth is patient-centered to its core. I can think of no better companion for the voyage than *The Unicorn Protocol* – and no better guide than Sally Ann Frank.

May these lessons light your path, fuel your courage, and one day inspire your own story of purposeful innovation.

Stephen Ibaraki
Investor, Futurist, Global Advisor and Mentor
Global Innovation and Startup Communities

Acknowledgments

Writing this book was very different from writing *The Startup Protocol*, because I am sharing other people's stories. This means that there are a TON more people to thank, starting with the Unicorn founders: Sean Duffy (Omada Health), Kevin Riddleberger (Dispatch Health), Abhinav Shashank (Innovaccer), Jonathan Bush (athenahealth), Jeff Elton (ConcertAI), Elad Walach (Aidoc), Roy Schoenberg (Amwell), Minhong Jang (Lunit), Niko Skievaski (Redox), and Molly He (Element Biosciences).

Not only were their contributions key to this effort, but as any founder – at any stage knows – keeping focused on the mission is essential, and this was definitely an extracurricular activity. Despite that, all ten of these founders found time to meet with me and review their chapters. Uniformly, they were gracious, brutally honest, and incredibly humble. I mean really humble.

Thank you all for entrusting me with your stories. It's a responsibility I have not taken lightly.

I would also like to thank those that trudged through the early version of the manuscript, providing helpful feedback, including Michael Greely, Flare Capital; Kathleen McGrow, Microsoft; Ali Tafreshi, Topcon Health; Gil Bashe, FINN Partners; Tom Lawry, Second City Tech; Mendel Erlenwein, CareCo; and Elliott Parker, Alloy Partners. Extra gratitude goes to Ranya Habash, MD, Bascom Palmer/University of Miami and CEO, Sweet Medical, and Aly Abayazeed, QradAI, for their painstaking review and helpful edits.

There were others that also helped tremendously along the way, including my friend and colleague Heena Purohit, who was my copilot for Copilot, helping me engineer prompts that would provide helpful insights and summaries of the transcripts that were used as raw materials for this book. I would also like to thank Tom Lawry, who continued to coach me through this book, as he had done while I wrote *The Startup Protocol.* His perspective and guidance were invaluable. Special thanks also go to Ariadna

Duran, who once again designed an intriguing cover for the book. Her talent and ability to translate my ramblings into a beautiful image astound me. Additionally, the terrific team at Taylor & Francis, led by amazing editor Kris Mednansky, was incredibly helpful, as always.

I'm also deeply appreciative of Stephen Ibaraki for writing the foreword. Stephen is constantly on the road, tirelessly contributing to the healthcare ecosystem on an almost unfathomable scale. His global perspective is truly a gift to everyone he knows, including me.

Lastly, I would like to thank my husband, Scott Buchanan, who once again was tasked with reviewing the first version of each chapter, painstakingly checking grammar, spelling, context, and readability. In addition, his encouragement, humor, and understanding as I spent too many weekends writing were essential in keeping me sane throughout the writing process. He is truly my biggest cheerleader. I'm so appreciative of his support and the support of the other members of my cheerleading squad, my mother, Mimi Frank, and my daughter, Brooke Phillips Miller. I love you all so very much!

About the Author

Sally Ann Frank leads the global healthcare and life sciences program for Microsoft for Startups, an organization dedicated to accelerating the development of innovative companies. Through business strategy, planning, go-to-market development, and technical excellence, she enables startups to achieve their revenue and long-term goals. Additionally, Sally directly mentors healthcare and life sciences founders at all stages of their company's development to help them thrive and positively impact the global healthcare delivery system. She also works directly with enterprise companies, VCs, accelerators, and other ecosystem players to facilitate connections, learning, and collaboration across the various stakeholders.

Previously, she was part of Microsoft's IoT Solutions team, helping healthcare and life sciences companies use IoT to improve patient outcomes and operational efficiencies. With more than 25 years in the technology industry, she is focused on business outcomes, helping providers, payers, medical device, pharmaceutical, and life sciences companies use, AI, machine learning, IoT, and other Microsoft technologies to meet the changing demands of the healthcare industry.

She earned an MBA from The George Washington University (Washington, DC), an MS in Systems Management from the University of Southern California, and a BS in Marketing with a minor in Computer Science from Virginia Tech. She is the author of *The Startup Protocol: A Guide for Digital Health Startups to Bypass Pitfalls and Adopt Strategies That Work*, published by Routledge.

She lives in the Charlotte, NC, metro area with her husband and her seven-pound Chihuahua.

Introduction

No one starts a healthcare or life sciences company because they think it's easy. They may not know just how hard it is, but they know it isn't easy. Frankly, that's why I love this industry. The people and these founders are mission-driven in ways that you don't see in other industries. Often driven by personal (undesirable) experiences with our healthcare system, as a clinician or patient or loved one of a patient, these founders are motivated to try to fix how we deliver healthcare. Personally, I like to think that I'm motivated to work out and eat right (mostly), but their degree of motivation is on a different plane. While many learned on the job, they were driven to do whatever was necessary to overcome obstacles, develop new markets, and positively impact healthcare.

Documenting their journeys required listening to their origin stories multiple times: once when I interviewed the founders (and in the case of Aidoc, I interviewed Elad Walach twice because the transcription failed the first time); another time when I turned the transcription into a readable form; and lastly when I edited the chapters (a few times) to ensure readability. Each time I went through a chapter, I could almost hear the founders in my head as they talked about milestones, mishaps, and management styles. Each time, I fell in love with their passion, fortitude, and occasional foibles.

The true-life stories you are about to read are compelling and deeply personal. In fact, after coming up with the concept for this book, I was concerned that founders would not want to share their stories. I was wrong – very wrong, in fact. In every case, as you will see, the founders were eager to share, and not because they wanted to stroke their own egos. They agreed to participate because they wanted to help other founders learn from their mistakes, good decisions, and everything in between. These founders are keenly aware that no single organization or person can fix healthcare. They want to be a part of the solution, in whatever form that takes.

It's probably a good time to define the term Unicorn. A Unicorn company is a privately owned startup that has been valued at more than $1 billion.[1] According to Failory, healthcare Unicorns constitute just 8% of all Unicorns and across all industries, the United States and China are the most prolific Unicorn producers.[2] According to CB Insights, their Unicorn Tracker now lists 1,283 Unicorns worldwide, with a total cumulative valuation of about $4.5 billion.[3] At this point, you are probably saying to yourself, "What's the likelihood that my company will become a Unicorn?" Well, the numbers vary, but they are not encouraging. According to CB Insights, there's a 1.28% chance.[4] According to Halle Tecco, founder of Rock Health, it's worse – just a 0.00006% chance.[5] But before you put this book down and search for another line of work, remember that becoming a Unicorn is not the only path to, or recognition of, success. While it may seem like the pinnacle, many founders and companies are positively affecting healthcare without reaching that $1 billion valuation mark.

With that background, my goal is to provide a holistic view of the startup founder journey from a variety of perspectives. I was able to

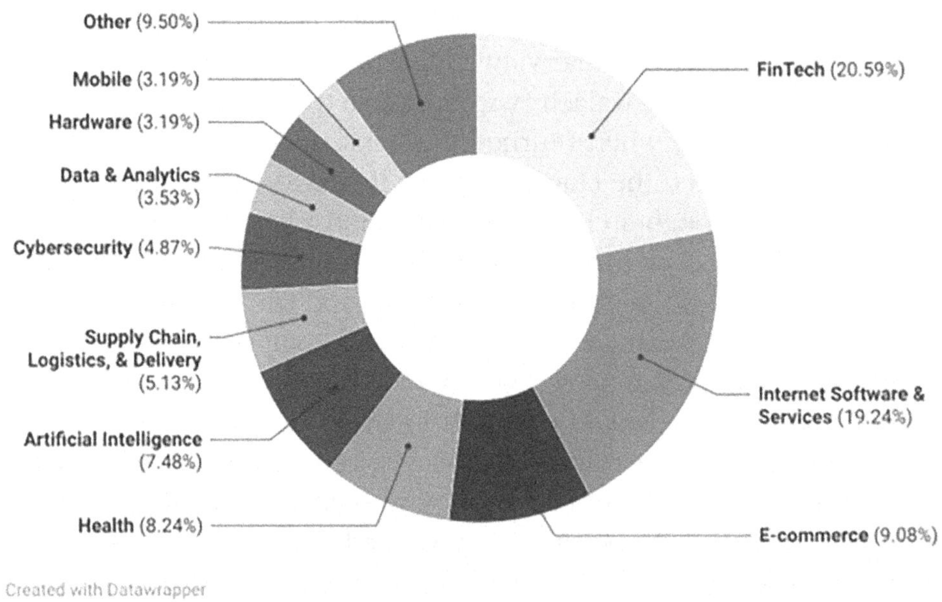

Unicorns by Industry (as of 2023)

Graphic courtesy of Failory.com https://www.failory.com/unicorns

interview Unicorn founders from India, South Korea, China, and Israel, with the balance from the United States. Since I work at Microsoft, it's important to note that many of these companies didn't participate in the Microsoft for Startups program. I intentionally identified category-leading startups, regardless of their chosen technology platform. More importantly, the technology selected is not a leading indicator of success (much to the chagrin of the three major cloud vendors).

Following the framework introduçed in *The Startup Protocol*, each chapter describes the company's development along the four major phases: Ideate, Build, Launch, and Grow. Using Copilot, I was able to use the four-phase framework to summarize each company's journey in the TLDR (Too Long Didn't Read) section of each chapter. Not to sound self-serving, I do recommend you read *The Startup Protocol* first, as it's designed to help early-stage founders with helpful strategies and tactical recommendations as the company is being formed. Additionally, *The Unicorn Protocol* may be more useful for founders and their teams who have already started building and are eager to understand the trajectory of successful startups that have gone before them.

Please note that as you read each founder's story, it is told from their perspective, with their words, edited for clarity. When you see "I," it refers to the founder, and the "we" refers to his or her team. I thought it was incredibly important to keep the tone and tenor for each founder intact so that you, the reader, feel like you are hearing the founder directly. That may also be reflected in sentence structure and word choices, as English is a second (or third) language for a few of the founders.

My hope is that as you read these stories, you will underline passages and make notes in the space at the end of each chapter so that you can refer, again and again, to parts of the stories that seem especially relevant to you. There's no magic here, but there are lessons that may be valuable to you on your journey. Who knows? One day, your company may reach Unicorn status, and people will ask you, "How did you do it?"

Endnotes

1 https://www.britannica.com/money/what-is-a-unicorn-startup
2 https://www.failory.com/unicorns
3 https://www.cbinsights.com/research-unicorn-companies
4 https://app.cbinsights.com/research/unicorn-conversion-rate
5 https://www.halletecco.com/blog/digital-health-unicorns

Chapter 1

Aidoc

It's not just about the performance of AI, but the value that it delivers.

– Elad Walach, Co-founder, CEO

1.1 Quick Facts

Website	https://www.aidoc.com/
Founded	2016
Mission	*We are a pioneering force in clinical AI, focusing on aiding and empowering healthcare teams to optimize patient treatment, resulting in improved economic value and clinical outcomes. Powered by Aidoc's exclusive aiOS™, we analyze and aggregate medical data that enables care teams to operationalize the unexpected and work seamlessly with a continued focus on the patient. Aidoc AI is always on, running in the background to change the foreground.*[1]
Founders	Elad Walach https://www.linkedin.com/in/elad-walach/ Michael Braginsky https://www.linkedin.com/in/michael-b-braginsky-72885616/ Guy Reiner https://www.linkedin.com/in/guy-reiner/ Gal Yaniv, PhD https://www.linkedin.com/in/gal-yaniv-54775837/

DOI: 10.4324/9781032711034-1

Unicorn status achieved	February 2025
Funding rounds[2]	Ten funding deals • September 2016–November 2023 • $6 million–$110 million
Notable funders	• General Catalyst • Emerge Ventures • Jibe Ventures

1.2 TLDR

Ideate

- Founded with a mission to address the high rate of misdiagnosis in the United States, which accounts for 375,000 deaths annually
- Focus on leveraging Artificial Intelligence (AI) to sift through massive amounts of unstructured healthcare data and coordinate care effectively
- The initial vision evolved from focusing solely on radiology to addressing end-to-end care pathways
- Emphasis on breaking down silos and providing a holistic view of the patient to improve quality of care

Build

- Developed the first product with a focus on workflow integration and high engagement
- Employed the lean startup methodology to test and validate the product with dozens of physicians
- Faced challenges with data normalization and workflow integration, leading to significant investments in platform development
- Built a strong R&D team and focused on customer success from the early stages

Launch

- Launched the first product after over a year of development, focusing on acute findings in radiology

- Achieved early adoption by working closely with customers and ensuring the product met their needs
- Conducted clinical validation and navigated the regulatory journey, including obtaining FDA (Food and Drug Administration) clearances
- Emphasized the importance of integrating AI into clinical workflows to ensure high engagement and usability

Grow

- Expanded from radiology to cardiology and neurology, maintaining a focus on delivering value and solving real problems
- Developed a strategy to sell a unified solution to health systems, targeting the C-suite for broader adoption
- Achieved significant milestones, including helping 10,000 patients a day and reaching 100,000 patients a day
- Maintained a focus on mission-based milestones, emphasizing the impact on patient care over financial metrics

1.3 Meet the Founder

Elad Walach

Elad Walach is a pioneering force in the field of clinical AI. As the co-founder and CEO of Aidoc, he has transformed AI in healthcare from a promising concept into a mission-critical solution that helps reduce diagnostic errors, close preventable care gaps, and support clinical teams at scale.

Since founding Aidoc in 2016, Elad has raised over $300 million in capital, built a global team of more than 500 employees, and introduced over 20 AI-powered solutions, including the most FDA-cleared clinical AI solutions on the market. Today, Aidoc supports care for more than 100,000 patients every day across 1,500 hospitals, delivering real-time intelligence to clinicians that enables improved outcomes, reduces clinician burnout, and drives smarter, more efficient care.

Recognized by *Modern Healthcare*'s 40 Under 40 and *Forbes*' 30 Under 30, Elad is also a sought-after global speaker, known for making complex AI concepts practical and actionable for healthcare and business leaders alike.

A graduate of The Hebrew University of Jerusalem with a background in mathematics and physics, Elad has authored multiple academic publications in deep learning. His work continues to advance the role of AI in healthcare with a focus on delivering on a bold vision to improve care through smarter, more connected decision-making.

1.4 Interview with Elad Walach, Co-founder and CEO

In preparing for our discussion, I looked at the data [Johns] Hopkins released from a study last year, and they found out that every year in the United States, there are about 400,000 deaths due to misdiagnosis. That is the third highest cause of death. That is one-eighth of all deaths in the United States. That is more than accidents and injuries, and it is all preventable. That is the crazy thing. We can prevent this problem, and it stems from the increasing complexity we have in healthcare.

> ***But the problem is that with this specialization, we're losing the patient.***

And what do big healthcare systems do all day long? They specialize. You have the neuro cancer specialist for a sub disease. But the problem is that with this specialization, we're losing the patient. We're treating a symptom, not the patient. And you see these fragmentation and coordination issues happening all the time. Here's an example. Let's say you get an imaging study, you get a report, and there is suspicion of cancer or an aneurysm. You [the patient] should follow up about that. But do you know the likelihood of a patient following up? Less than 50%. *Less than 50%.* Why is that? It's because, for the people who originally treated you for something, these recommendations are incidental. They are treating one thing, and then they find the suspected cancer or aneurysm, and they cannot coordinate care. People who know how to treat cancer or aneurysms do not get to the patient.

I think that is the systemic issue we have in healthcare: this fragmentation of everything, of incentives, of data, of physicians. We need to somehow break this vicious cycle. An additional statistic that was, for me, really troubling to see is the productivity of healthcare. Healthcare is the only industry that has lost productivity in the last two decades – it's crazy. We're becoming less efficient on a per capita basis, and yet in every other industry where technology has helped, we are more productive. Healthcare is the only one that has not improved.

So, the premise is that we have this mega industry, 20% of US GDP, that is on the brink of collapse because of inefficiency. We must find a different way to solve this with data. I think we all believe that AI is part of that cure because AI has the potential to sift through the massive amounts of unstructured data we have and find the right signal. And then we can coordinate the signal to the right physician, for the right patient, at the right time, and we see that happening all the time. But the problem was – and I think this is why Aidoc came to be – the problem was the same fragmentation issue when applying AI. The way it works, you need to get an FDA clearance per disease, so there were 900 FDA clearances.

We were trying to solve this problem of fragmentation.

So, effectively, what happened was that we were trying to solve this problem of fragmentation. We all know that you can fight fire with fire, but you don't fix fragmentation with more fragmentation. That was a big problem, and we wanted to solve this problem. That is the premise of Aidoc, building that platform. Yes, we have applications, but the end goal is that they are all connected into one layer to break down silos, provide a holistic view of the patient, and massively improve the quality of care.

Our vision for the company evolved in the context of growing from one service line to many. We originally thought about this exact approach, but in radiology. We said we want to be <u>the</u> imaging AI platform. It took us a while to realize that it was the wrong question to ask because the patient is not an image, and you need to think about the end-to-end care pathway. But it took us a long time to develop that type of vision. Part of it was we thought tackling this problem may be too big for one company. We had to really mature and grow into being able to deliver. So, our vision did evolve, but it was based on the same premise.

Going back to the MVP, originally, we thought that the company would be much more of an algorithm company. We'd develop the algorithms, and then the value would be very obvious; everybody would use them. And then the importance of the workflow really hit us. We were three tech founders, right?

So, coming back to the founding story, I was head of an AI department for the Israeli Air Force. My two co-founders were in a special unit, Talpiot, which is very well known. Investors trusted our technical expertise without question. Fine, we can build it. But is it usable, and does it solve the business need? That was the key question.

> ***A lot of our early days building the MVP were focused on knowing if the solution solved the problem.***

A lot of our early days building the MVP were focused on knowing if the solution solved the problem. We used the lean startup methodology. We had a bunch of ideas, and Aidoc was number four on the list. The other ideas just failed. We developed a mockup that *simulated* AI, but it wasn't really AI. We had dozens and dozens of physicians, like sitting with the mockup, and we wanted to reach a point where they would tell us, "Hey, if this works, I need this yesterday!" And that is the type of response we got when we showed them the idea of Aidoc, but again, it never actually worked right. It was just us mocking up everything, trying to clarify the problem being solved.

> ***I think it took us more than a year to get the first product into production.***

I think developing the first product, especially in healthcare, is very complex. In many industries, you move fast and build a mockup, and the quality doesn't matter that much because you are just getting early feedback. In healthcare, you don't have as many chances because of the needed accuracy. You can lose a brand and trust very quickly. So, we worked very hard – I think it took us more than a year to get the first product into production. We had to develop the algorithm, and developing the workflow integration was really a key piece of it.

When we did our first installation, it was about how do we create the best workflow experience. I think that was the key piece for us; we were obsessive about understanding our customers and being with them. We didn't release it into the workflow and leave it alone. We had people on site for weeks just looking and observing how they use it. And we learned a lot of interesting lessons from that period.

I'll give you one lesson from the platform side: we learned firsthand that there is this weird data normalization problem in healthcare. In healthcare data, we all say it's unstructured. But even when you think it's structured like imaging, it's apparently unstructured. For example, there is no easy way of knowing if, according to the metadata, an image of the head is actually an image of the head, which is weird. Apparently, the fact that it's a head image is not in the metadata. That information is manually configured. When we saw that they were relying on humans to do the mapping and what we call the problem of orchestration, it started failing because the protocols for how they image patients kept changing all the time. As a result, our system started failing, and the AI would miss – not because the AI would miss, but because the data model changed under it. That was a lesson that could only be uncovered if you're in there and see how these protocols change over time.

The clinical validation process has also really changed over time.

The clinical validation process has also really changed over time. I likened it to the way a person watches TV shows. In the early days, there were only a few TV shows, right? When you thought about watching something, you would say, "OK, let me look at the trailers and the reviews and if I like it, maybe I'll watch an episode or a pilot." If I liked it, I would buy it. It was the same way with the early AI models in that they would validate the model. Typically, they would send us scans retrospectively and would have us validate them. But it really changed over time, and because we now have so many of them at the same time, the topic of data drift is very meaningful.

Even if I show you the model works today, there's nothing that promises it will continue to work over time. So, the validation process has changed from what was called an FDA language pre-market[3] to a monitoring and post-market model[4] where it needs to be governed over time. And that governance is part of the benefit of having a platform – you can invest in this infrastructure layer.

Validation is an incredibly important topic, and I think vendors need to take this very, very seriously. We see again and again that if you don't continue to monitor the model, you can easily have drift and lose as much as 10% accuracy within a year. In terms of regulation, the FDA is obviously a key part of clinical AI. There are lots of spaces evolving right now that don't necessarily require clearance yet. But clinical AI, like clinical decision-making, oftentimes requires clearance. That means we must go through the process, and as a result, the models (today, at least) are typically frozen. If I want to change it, I need to go through an FDA clearance process. It's not automatic because, for clinical applications, everything needs to be validated 1,000 times.

Moving on from regulation to integrating our models into workflows, we had developed a kind of mental framework with three layers. Layer number one is the algorithm. We needed to have high-performing algorithms, and you measure that by accuracy. The second layer is a working product, so you need to look at the workflow and make sure that there is high engagement, measured by its actual usage. The third layer on top is the solution. You need to identify a clear pain point, have a clear value, and measure the impact that the solution has on a problem. Those three layers are all necessary to deliver a product that creates value, and a lot of founders focus too much on the algorithm and the technical side, but not enough on the solution side.

> ***In the early days we met with a neuroradiologist who told us that workflow is primary and that he didn't have time for additional button clicks. We told him, "That's fine – just one button click and you'll get the results." And then he said, "Guys, you're not listening. Not one button click, I mean ZERO button clicks."***

In the early days we met with a neuroradiologist who told us that workflow is primary and that he didn't have time for additional button clicks. We told him, "That's fine – just one button click and you'll get the results." And then he said, "Guys, you're not listening. Not one button click, I mean ZERO button clicks." That was the challenge we had, and honestly, it was the best advice we ever got because nobody wants to click an extra button. They're all too busy already. We had to find a way to make that happen. The way we operate is what we call contextual awareness, so the platform is aware of the user's actions and then presents the relevant information. The easiest way to think about it is like a Dropbox icon or notification on a mobile app instead of opening an app and then typing. This was just another facet of our relentless focus on our customers.

The key to the user experience is knowing what you want, and then giving it to you at the right moment is critical. To do that, we had to develop integrations across many, many systems in the ecosystem. I think there were about ten different systems. And again, people think about AI and our company, and it is true that we have the most everyday clearances. We have about 20 FDA clearances, and I'm still telling you we spent more on the platform side – in the tens of millions of US dollars, if not more. We probably spent more than $100 million on all the aspects of the platform, from data normalization to monitoring the data and models to managing the integration.

In terms of scaling to multiple models, I will say it is very challenging. Even if you know it's challenging and try to prepare, it still catches you by surprise. Because, in the early days of a startup, you are used to knowing everything, and it's very easy to be agile and make decisions. However, when you have multiple product lines, which then leads to multiple user segments, it gets complicated. When we sell to cardiology departments, they don't know Aidoc from radiology; they don't know us from neuroscience. Each service line is its own segment, and they go to their own conferences and read their own journals. So, it becomes very difficult to become an expert and a known entity in all of them. As a result, we began to specialize and ended up with the same problem internally as they have in healthcare – everyone is a specialist. We still have growing pains because it's hard to build the organization to do all of this. It's everything from how our sales team operates in the field and whether they have the support they need to how we develop products. Every level of the organization needs to change from this one focused entity to multiple service lines, and then how they speak together. I think a big part of that is having developed a strategy that combined everything. I do not see us as a company that sells three different, distinct product lines to three different entities. It's one solution to a health system that has three different products. But to accomplish this, we had to develop this broader strategy internally as well as externally so we could sell to the C-suite of the health system.

I would only recommend building multiple services lines if you have a strong enough base, like we had.

That was a very big evolution for us that I think is interesting for a lot of companies. We've seen a lot of companies fail at scaling because you must be very good at several things at once to achieve scale. I would only recommend building multiple service lines if you have a strong enough base, like we had. For example, we were strong enough in radiology that we could leverage that work and experience, feeling confident that we're not stretching ourselves too thin. And even when we are focused on growth, we're also very focused on targeting only one or two service lines at a time.

We're not trying to boil the ocean all at once. It's just impossible. I know it's very common advice, but focus for a startup is so, so key – not only on what you plan to do, but also, more importantly, on what you're not going to do.

With these different service lines, we now need to get to the C-suite of a hospital to sell the platform and how it supports those three service lines. And this type of growth is materially different because you are essentially selling a different product to a different user segment. Even if it was the same product, you must position it differently. This approach isn't a fit for every company. For some companies, it's better to segment and sell to different service lines. In our case, I think it made a lot of sense to create a unified, centralized strategy. I will say we were also fortunate with the timing, as AI became much more of a strategic initiative. So even selling the same story two years ago would have been more difficult than it is today.

I'm also fortunate to be invited, on a weekly basis, to present to executive teams or a board of a health system to help them get a grasp on how AI can help them. And I think it's good because we're educating the market in the right way. But the bottom line is, it's very, very complex and not always the right fit for every company. We earned the right by having a great product for at least one service line. We earned the right by tackling a big enough problem for the health system. It's not a low-ticket item or point solution, because we had multiple service lines involved. We have earned the right to go to the C-suite. And once you earn it, I think you can sell a strategy or transformation play versus a point solution plan, which was our mission all along.

> ***It's about changing, with AI being a tool that enables you to do change management in your health system. But to do that, you need leadership, clinical operational leadership within the health system.***

Today, it's both good and bad that our target C-suite persona is very diverse, because if you ask most health systems who runs their AI strategy, you'll get diverse answers. It could be the chief medical officer (CMO) or chief clinical officer for some health system. The chief information officer (CIO) is very common, as is the chief digital officer (CDO), as more systems start hiring that type of position. Others have hired a chief AI officer, and sometimes the CEO is very interested. Unfortunately, I don't have a "one-size-fits-all" approach. It's more dependent on one leader who has a vision for transformation. It can be someone wearing the innovation hat because he or she understands the potential of this to their business. It turns out to be less about the title and more about the personality and the goals of that particular person. It's also about organizational dynamics and who's strong enough to lead the initiative. I saw the importance of having clear leaders on the other side – people who can actually lead change. Because if you really want to optimize, in my mind, it's wrong to think about it as adopting AI. It's about changing, with AI being a tool that enables you to do change management in your health system. But to do that, you need leadership, clinical operational leadership within the health system.

Change management was one of the most important things as we expanded beyond one service line. When you go across functional areas, all these change management elements and issues are multiplied 100-fold. We saw some adoption hurdles in the early days when we went through these cross-functional departments. People loved the product but didn't know how to adopt it or convince other stakeholders to adopt it.

And then we built this solution success framework and a team to go work with our customers to do the change management. As a result, we saw adoption rates literally double, if not more, in some cases. So, purposeful change management does really help. Another element is that people sometimes assume that if you give customers the product, then they'll immediately understand the value. I found that even if people really like something, they may not fully internalize how beneficial it is. So, the value extraction concept became part of our success process, where we helped our customers and partners to review the data, find the metrics they cared about, and measure the success enterprise-wide.

Field engagement is not sufficient in the current environment. You must show them why it's making a difference. A friend and a mentor of mine, Stephen Klasko, the former CEO of Jefferson Health, shared an analogy that I really liked. He said,

> *I'm having a heart attack right now. If you come to me and tell me, hey, I have this amazing idea about how to renovate your kitchen. I would tell you, you know, get the hell out of here, right? But if you find me a cure for heart disease then I know I need this and want to talk.*
>
> *It's not just about the performance of AI, but the value that it delivers.*

AI should be positioned not as "Let's renovate your kitchen." But instead, let's find you treatment. I think that's the primary goal: focus on value and how we transform the business and show that both during and after implementation. It's not just about the performance of AI but the value that it delivers.

For us, the big move to unlocking value was doing a retrospective study and baselining because it's a bit harder for us to measure value. Sometimes it's possible to measure value on an ongoing basis, but at other times you compare pre- and post-implementation results. We opted to do the latter, which allowed us to do things like ROI measurement and stuff like that. And that was very effective.

Another thing was measuring value on an ongoing basis. For us, that meant finding patient stories and sharing them, which is super important. We also encouraged our customers to share as well. At the end of the day, this is about impacting patients, and if you have these amazing stories, it's worthwhile sharing them.

When we began to expand significantly, focus was key. While we had this big, bold vision, it was important to pace ourselves and focus. In the early days, our focus was radiology, specifically acute findings and radiology. (Afterward, we went to the ambulatory, but initially, we were just working on acute inpatient findings.) Radiology was the initial focus, and we executed relentlessly, growing our customer base and brand within radiology. It took us a few years.

> ***From that point, we just paced ourselves and every year we asked the same question: are we ready and if so, how many new products are we going to bite off this year.***

I would say when we reached a mass of, say, over $10 million of annual recurring revenue (ARR) or something like that, we got to a point where we said, "OK, we have enough of a foothold, and we feel secure enough that we can allow ourselves to start expanding our scope." There are always challenges, but we felt good enough that we could start broadening our offerings. We picked two service lines, cardio and neuro, and expanded there. From that point, we just paced ourselves, and every year we asked the same question: are we ready, and if so, how many new products are we going to bite off this year? But it was a lengthy process, and I think it will continue to be. We tell our system partners, "Partner with us because you like our current offering, but know that you are also signing up for a journey." It's not buying a product, right? We tell them, "We're going to work on it together and evolve over the years. And the Aidoc you have three years from now is going to look nothing like the Aidoc you have today." Hopefully, those who have been with us for the last few years can attest to that point. It's really about the ongoing evolution.

While growth is great, one of my goals is to avoid imploding because we grew too quickly. It's important to measure burn, even if you raise funds. We raised a lot of money in our day. But you can't let it get to your head; be very conservative and spend carefully. We've been intentional with our burn rate and remain on a clear path to break even. I think that's one thing I would encourage – balancing profitable growth.

We were always measuring burn and had this culture of humility – not excessive frugality but focusing on what matters.

When we raised money, the market was very good, but we still wanted to be conservative, so you would never see us doing massive rave parties or sending people to private islands. We were always measuring burn and had this culture of humility – not excessive frugality but focusing on what matters. That was instrumental in helping us moderate our spending. So, I think just being reasonable on our spending, not letting the fact that we had cash at one point in time, and preparing for Black Swan events are all key concepts for managed growth.

So, it ends up being focused on delivering value.

Another important thing, coming back to focus, and maybe it's even a weakness of us as a company, but early on, we were very much in the weeds on details. While other companies pursue the Big Bang healthcare product, going from above and selling this massive vision, we grew from a small use case and added one use case at a time. It took us a while to, what we would call, earn the right to come with a vision that is backed up by data and more than 100 clinical studies. It's a very different approach and one that I think our customers really value. So, it ends up being focused on delivering value. Don't mislead yourself, buying your own stories about how we're going to change the world. I think that was a key aspect of our growth and still is.

I think if I had to pick, I'd rather be a product company that can improve our go-to-market execution than the reverse. Strategically speaking, that approach puts us in a very good spot.

We are also a very R&D-heavy company. Ratio-wise, we're probably investing more in R&D than most companies that I know of. And I think part of it is because we have so much to build, unlike other businesses where you build something and then focus on selling the thing they built. They don't have as much development as we do. Strategically, at our core, we're always going to be much more R&D heavy, but that also drives the talent that gets hired. Our first-year hires were in customer success. It was not sales. Customer success and R&D – those were the things that we focused on, especially in the early days of building our team. We only brought the go-to-market later, and I would argue that we're still catching up, developing our go-to-market function. But I'm fine with that. I think if I had to pick, I'd rather be a product company that can improve our go-to-market execution than the reverse. Strategically speaking, that approach puts us in a very good spot.

We wanted to raise a seed round early. Medical devices are expensive and could cost millions of dollars. I will say the seed round was especially challenging for us because it was in the early days of digital health. Most VCs, especially in Israel, didn't really know what health was, and were afraid of it as a target industry. I think we were one of the earlier digital health investments in Israel, which was very challenging. It took us about a year. (Hopefully, that encourages people to stick with it.) In the early days, we got about 100 "No's" from VCs. At that point in time, many people didn't want to hear about healthcare. They were confused about the industry. I remember one VC who told us after a conversation, "Guys, you look like a great team. Why would you waste your time in the healthcare space? It's not a big problem to solve and it's a confusing market."

Obviously, I'm still happy that we stayed in healthcare. So that was the seed, and it did become a bit easier after that. Over the next couple of years, we had the A & B, and they were mainly fueled by the early pilots and engagement success, not commercial success. We were able to show how the product was really going viral and that people loved it. Since then, because product success translated to commercial success, we were able to attract very good C & D investors, including General Catalyst in the C round and TCV in the D round, and that helped us grow.

> ***But in those early days, when we were raising our seed round, we didn't even have a customer. We had maybe a letter of intent from a customer. We couldn't just go and build it because it was too costly to develop.***

But in those early days, when we were raising our seed round, we didn't even have a customer. We had maybe a letter of intent from a customer. We couldn't just go and build it because it was too costly to develop. We were pre-customer, but we had some intent as well as KOLs [key opinion leaders] who had validated and liked the idea. However, it was less than a year between our seed round and our A round. We were very fortunate to have met our A round investor, as she really bought into the vision, so it was more of a preemptive round. We didn't have to raise in the conventional sense. So, we took the money, and that helped us accelerate. And then it was about a year and a half to the B round, I think.

Regarding our technology, I'll say one thing – we're very lucky that we're tech founders. We had access to a lot of great tech talent and just built it. The stack we chose was mainly based on AWS. They were our early partners, and we found them to be the best for AI development, in terms of the maturity of their stack. But I don't think that was the key. I will say that our tech focus, from early on, was on building the solution, not on the science. It's not to say that we weren't doing tech breakthroughs, because we were (and are). We're solving a lot of interesting, complex problems, but it's always from the vantage point of productizing. I think tech teams in AI occasionally over-focus on developing these cool models but not on solving a real problem.

I'll give you an example – the monitoring platform we developed early on is key to managing data drift. It's not a sexy problem to solve, but data drift must be removed. I think people want to develop these cool models, but nobody cares about your model if the data feeding it changes all the time, and you're not analyzing 30% of cases. And when we tried to problem-solve again, it was never just about the AI. The stack was around everything from how you run experiments to how you monitor them to how you normalize data – the whole chain.

Even as we become more successful, we're still always thinking and a bit scared about what's next. We're always focused on the next challenge. And my chief business officer and I would meet and say, "We just need to reach $1M in sales," and then it's, "We need to reach $5M. . . ." Then we need to move to $10 million. But that's product market fit; it's never-ending. And even now, we're aiming for $200 million.

It always feels like we have a lot more to go, but on the flip side, I always had a conviction about the vision. I think it was sometime last year when I was thinking, "Holy cow! This is actually making a massive impact." I think that happened as we reached roughly 10,000 patients a day. That's big, right? That's a lot of people. And now we're at the pace of 100,000 a day, which is pretty crazy.

> ***I got excited knowing we had achieved something based on how many patients we've helped. It's the impact of those things that make me tick.***

For one month, we had a lot of [clinical validation] papers that came in at the same time. We had a paper from Sheba Hospital in Israel showing about a 30% reduction in mortality. Another paper came in from Cedars-Sinai showing a reduction in length of stay. All of this came together, and I was like, wow, we're solving a big problem at scale. I got excited knowing we had achieved something based on how many patients we've helped. It's the impact of those things that make me tick. This whole Unicorn thing, honestly, I don't like it. I mean, the journey is not done. It's not done, so it practically means nothing. I think the key thing is how many people you helped. In that sense, even if we failed tomorrow morning, I would still be satisfied, because we helped a lot of people. (And, of course, I don't want that to happen!) The traditional measures of success, funds raised, and Unicorn status all feel like vanity metrics of the journey. Look, I can fundraise and hire twice as many people tomorrow morning. Obviously, it's good to have a high valuation because it helps you with funding. But in and of itself, it is not a meaningful metric.

I'd also like to say that I'm very happy this book is being written for digital health. I think healthcare needs help, and I know healthcare is a very daunting space. People are afraid to pursue it and, to some extent, for good reason. It's a very tough nut to crack, but the healthcare space has one of the highest returns. I think it's perhaps the highest. And if you solve an actual problem, then you're very sticky. I would encourage people to think about solving big problems. And to be clear, if people just want to develop something and then sell it, that's also absolutely fine. I have no judgment about that, but I think we need entrepreneurs to tackle big problems, to change the face of healthcare. We need it. Our screwed-up healthcare system is not going away. And I do not think we can rely on political change. I mean, I hope we'll have a government-led change. But more realistically, I think we're going to be stuck in the same fragmented environment and technology. The only way out is a massive increase in productivity. So, here's a call to action to anybody who can come to this space and solve big problems.

1.5 Notes

Endnotes

1 Meet Aidoc: Your Partner in Healthcare AI Solutions.
2 https://my.pitchbook.com/profile/169854-94/company/profile
3 More on pre-market approvals; https://www.fda.gov/medical-devices/premarket-submissions-selecting-and-preparing-correct-submission/premarket-approval-pma
4 More on post-market regulations; https://www.fda.gov/medical-devices/medical-device-regulatory-science-research-programs-conducted-osel/methods-and-tools-effective-postmarket-monitoring-artificial-intelligence-ai-enabled-medical-devices

Chapter 2

Amwell

But the decision to work alongside others and understand that we were only going to be successful if we made our customers successful – our success was through them – was one of the best decisions we made.

– Roy Schoenberg, Co-founder and Chairman

2.1 Quick Facts

Websites	https://patients.amwell.com/ https://business.amwell.com/
Founded	2006
Mission	*We digitally empower our clients' healthcare ambitions. We bring together technology, services, and devices into a connected ecosystem of care that improves the clinician experience and provides better patient access throughout the care continuum.*[1]
Founders	Roy Schoenberg https://www.linkedin.com/in/royschoenberg/ Ido Schoenberg https://www.linkedin.com/in/ido-schoenberg-80711779/

DOI: 10.4324/9781032711034-2

Unicorn status achieved	September 2020
Funding rounds[2]	Ten funding deals • February 2007–January 2021 • $31 million–$310 million
Notable funders	• Northwell Holdings • Takeda Pharmaceuticals • Gaia Holdings

2.2 TLDR

Ideate

- Founded by Roy Schoenberg and Ido Schoenberg in 2006
- Concept inspired by online dating apps, focusing on matching patients with available clinicians
- Initial idea emerged after selling their previous company, CareKey
- Aim to create a switchboard for healthcare, leveraging technology to connect patients and clinicians

Build

- Quickly secured seed and Series A funding, raising around $50 million
- Developed and patented the concept of brokering time with available clinicians
- Partnered with Blue Cross Blue Shield of Hawaii as the first client
- Faced significant opposition from medical boards but gained support from state governments

Launch

- Launched the first product in 2008, before the introduction of the iPhone
- Expanded to other payers like WellPoint (now Anthem) and United Optum
- Built a network of clinicians across all 50 states, ensuring 24/7 availability
- Transitioned to cloud-based infrastructure during COVID-19 to handle increased demand

Grow

- Went public during COVID-19, leveraging the increased demand for telehealth
- Developed a new platform, Converge, to support the evolving needs of telehealth
- Expanded internationally through acquisitions and partnerships
- Continued to innovate and adapt to changing healthcare landscapes, focusing on logistics and patient experience

2.3 Meet the Founder

Roy Schoenberg

Roy is a serial health-tech entrepreneur. After founding and running both private and public companies (now into his fourth venture), Roy's impact can be easily traced to everything from tele-ICU to patient portals, the introduction of telehealth, and now AI's arrival into healthcare. He worked closely with leaders of our largest health systems, national and regional payers, blue-chip tech companies, state and federal agencies, and policymakers both in Washington and overseas.

After founding and running Amwell as CEO for 18 years, Roy transitioned to an executive board position so he could focus on his next disruption – a novel model for the use of AI for caregiving and elder companionship. His groundbreaking ideas in this area have already captured the industry's imagination, as evident in the recent *New England Journal of Medicine Catalyst* publication.

Outside of his entrepreneurial endeavors, Roy chairs the MIT Sloan HSI healthcare advisory board. He is a member of the American Heart Association telehealth board and his hometown Mass General Brigham Patient Safety Research and Practice board. Previously, Roy served on the board of the American Telemedicine Association, where he was honored with the industry leadership award. He was inducted into the University of California at San Francisco (UCSF) Hall of Fame and repeatedly recognized by Modern Healthcare magazine as one of the 100 Most Influential People in Healthcare.

Roy holds an MD from The Hebrew University and an MPH from Harvard. He is happiest next to a whiteboard or a microphone, believes in creative provocation, owns more than 50 issued US patents, and divides his time between Boston and the island of Nantucket with his wife and two children.

2.4 Interview with Roy Schoenberg, Co-founder and Chairman

You know, if someone found the recipe showing how to do it in a way that is consistently successful, I'm pretty sure that book would sell like hotcakes. It's all about circumstances. In many cases, it's people and circumstances. But there are a lot of things that you shouldn't do. I think the things that you should do are, in many cases, opportunistic and depend on the environment, but there are things you shouldn't do, that's for sure.

As for our origin story, my brother and I do the businesses we do together. We had a couple of companies before. This was somewhere around 2006 when we had just sold our previous company to TriZetto Provider Solutions, and we were wondering what to do next. We took a break at the beach to figure out what to do. In all honesty, I was single at the time (this was many, many years ago), and I used a thing called Match.com.

Our previous company was all about patient portals and that kind of stuff, and the patient portals were very exciting to a lot of people. But people used them once, and then they never came back again. Now we know, 20 years later, that this didn't work. And I think the realization was that to most people, patient portals at the time were all about clinical content and health risk assessments and all that kind of stuff. To most people, this is not what healthcare means. To most people, very naively, healthcare means getting in front of a doctor. That's it.

When I was experiencing this early generation of the online dating app, it just occurred to us that it's just a supply and demand management system. It's a very cynical way of looking at online dating, but it really is. At any point in time, there are people who want to be available for that kind of thing, and there are people at the same time who are looking for availability. That's the magic, and it's also true about medicine as well. At any point in time, there are clinicians who are not in front of a patient. And at that same time, there are patients out there who could really benefit from getting in front of that clinician. But at the time, we didn't have a matchmaking capability. Long story short, that was the concept, and that was the idea – that was the part that was missing.

Technology had arrived at the point where we could create a switchboard for all of this. So, we said, "Let's go!" What we thought was going to be a couple of years of sitting at the beach and doing nothing ended up being about a month and a half. And then we are back in the saddle.

One of the good things about having this idea happened literally a month and a half after we sold our previous company successfully was that we knew a couple of people who were interested and somewhat happy with how we did the previous company. Furthermore, the previous company was also operating in the same environment as Amwell. We worked with a lot of health plans, clinicians, and so on, making it a very, very quick transition from there.

> ***I think the fact that this idea of brokering time with available clinicians resonated with people, not with investors. And at the end of the day, investors were just people, too.***

The first thing we did was write down the patent, which, crazily enough, was actually novel and was granted, which was wonderful. The next thing we did was go to the people we had worked with over the years, both by way of operations like the health plans and others, as well as investors, and we said to them, "Let's go for it, let's try and do this thing." I think the fact that this idea of brokering time with available clinicians resonated with *people*, not with investors. And at the end of the day, investors were just people, too.

That really helped us do a very quick seed round and a very quick A round. We made the case to them, even though at this time it was such a controversial model of delivering healthcare. There was no telehealth, and we said to them, "This is one of those cases where your investment will provide dividends in many years, but it will be a generational leap for how people experience healthcare." And I'm glad today that, in hindsight, telehealth really became something. But that was how it came to be. We contacted friends and family and people we had worked with in the past, and we were off to the races.

Our previous company was called Care Key, and we developed patient portals and member portals for health plans. We were very lucky that we developed this roughly around the time that Health Insurance Portability and Accountability Act (HIPAA) was enacted. Health plans realized, suddenly, that they needed to create a relationship with their membership to use the data. Under HIPAA, the health plans needed patient consent to use the data. And the Internet, invented by Al Gore, of course, seemed to be a very direct way to open that channel of communications that really didn't exist at the time. We had those web-based patient portals in place, and then they became popular right after HIPAA was enacted. It was a very favorable exit for us, so it worked well.

One of the nice things about it when we started to build was that there was no product. Additionally, I can tell you that if you talked to a couple of people back in 2006, the notion of a clinician caring for a patient and actually prescribing a medication or whatever without putting their hands or their stethoscope on the patient was heresy – a really terrible thing. So, there weren't a lot of people that were saying, "Oh, this is how it should work." There were, however, a lot of people who said, "This is why it's not going to work," which was also extremely valuable, to be clear. That feedback helped elevate the concerns, and we had to assume that the naysayers were going to lead the way.

We didn't know the extent to which that was going to happen. I can tell you that the first day that we rolled out our product was in 2008. Remember, this was a couple of months before the iPhone was introduced. Our first client was Blue Cross Blue Shield of Hawaii (Hawaii Medical Service Association (HMSA)).

And as you can imagine, their willingness to do this was driven by the fact that in the Hawaiian Islands, a lot of healthcare is in Honolulu, and a lot of people who live on other islands have no healthcare. They literally have to fly over to see their regular physician to get care. So, for them this was a very interesting proposition, as many people not having this would mean not getting care. It was an access issue that we were solving. But I want to give you a sense of how aggressive the opposition to telehealth was at the time.

On the day that we launched a product in collaboration with Blue Cross Blue Shield, which was a very large and powerful entity, the Hawaiian Medical Boards issued a public letter to all the physicians in Hawaii, telling them that if they're going to do this telehealth thing, they're going to take their license. And this is day one of your product as a young company.

Let me tell you something – this is how I got a lot of my gray hair!

> ***[O]ne thing that you learn, over the years of doing this, is this phrase that I like: nothing is as good or as bad as it initially seems.***

But look, one thing that you learn, over the years of doing this, is this phrase that I like: nothing is as good or as bad as it initially seems. You need to take a breath. Things do pan out a bit differently the next morning or a week later.

> ***I think the lesson learned here is that you really must choose well, who your launch partners are going to be.***

The opposition by the Hawaiian Medical Board was so aggressive, so draconian, that the governor and the Senate of Hawaii took interest and said, "Why are you poopooing this product from the get-go?" Long story short, two weeks later the Senate of the State of Hawaii passed a bill that *required* that every resident of Hawaii have access to healthcare through technology; essentially, the Senate overruled the medical board, which is a government entity. It was the first bill to be passed in the 50 states that embraced the notion of the validity of telehealth. From there, I can tell you stories, but things spiraled – in good ways. I think the lesson learned here is that you really must choose well who your launch partners are going to be. We did this with Blue Cross Blue Shield of Hawaii, who were courageous, literally. The leadership, the courage they displayed, because we know that Blue Cross health plans are usually not perceived as the most technologically innovative or anything else. But they took a gamble, and they said, "We need this to democratize access to healthcare, to people who are geographically separated."

They had a purpose in doing this, and they were the ones, as the prevailing health plan, that brought this to the attention of the governor and a variety of policymakers. They made their point, and they didn't chicken out. They said, "This makes no sense because what you're saying as a medical board, is that it is better for people have no access to healthcare than if they have access to healthcare through technology." And of course, that made no sense at all.

And by the way, I think this can be brought into today's world, and we can talk about where I think this technology should go. But at the time, the conversation was really about people's right to get healthcare, not about the various things that you should or shouldn't do through telehealth. It was about doing right by the people. It's very good to have a product that is on the side of doing right by the people, I'll tell you that. But we had to fight this battle with other customers on two fronts. One is to convince others, mostly health plans, and later, to convince health systems and so on that they should get into this as well, even though they don't have the geography of Hawaii, for example. But the reality is, you have the same reality in western Texas. You have the same reality in Minnesota or North Dakota in the winter. And you have urban deserts in New York that have no access to care. So, it became very easy to make the case that this technology opens up opportunities for people to get healthcare all over the country. The challenge was that every state has its own medical board. And working across states is an issue as well. To this day, if you are a clinician, you are not allowed to see a patient who is coming from another state. There are instruments today that help a little bit, but not by much. We spent the next five years, maybe more, going in front of medical boards in every state and making the case for telehealth. I can tell you that some states have been incredibly open and supportive, and some states have had staunch opposition to this for almost a decade after that. In some cases, there were concerns about the quality of care that would be delivered, and in some cases, it was Guild protection to make sure that the clinician in that state would not lose business because healthcare would travel via technology from other states. Every state had a different story; every state had a different adoption curve.

Going back to choosing the partners that you want to work with, the next two large customers that we had were WellPoint, which became Anthem/Elevance, and UHG/Optum. And of course, they are spread all over the country in so many ways. So, they became very good partners and went with us to the medical boards to make the case that their membership would get overall better care through this technology. That led to going to Capitol Hill and the White House together. Paul Ryan, the Speaker of the House at the time, was working and helping us. This product was really more about fulfilling the mission. Maybe in hindsight, we didn't even know it was going to be such a journey. But this is what it took to get people to be comfortable with our approach to telehealth.

I think it's safe to say that the first ten years or so were mostly focused on payers because for them, the governing principle is that people who have problems accessing care usually end up either doing nothing, which is really bad, or they end up going to the wrong care setting, like going to the ER when they don't really need to. So, if we can bring good healthcare to the payers' members, which means good clinicians who are trained and tested regularly, with quality certifications and positive secret shopping experiences, if we're able to deliver quality care, then this will help our membership. There were a lot of studies documenting real ROI for the payers. So, the first ten years were focused on the payers, and then we started working with health systems and hospitals. We realized that, in a way, they're getting into the payer business by taking the risk for patients. The first example of that was the readmission period, when the provider is penalized if a patient gets readmitted. Providers started thinking,

> *If we're responsible for the well-being of a patient when they leave our facility, then we need to check up on them. And we can do a better job of this if we use technology. The right technology translates into less risk.*

Additionally, providers wanted to get better margins and improve financial outcomes. All of this made a lot of health systems pick up telehealth, mostly for outpatient and post-discharge.

And then COVID-19 arrived.

During COVID-19, I would say even to this day, a lot of health systems got devastated because they couldn't see patients. Anything that was not lifesaving was locked down. And since the vast majority of health systems make money by submitting claims for seeing patients, and they weren't seeing patients, it was awful. It was a nightmare for most hospitals. And then they realized that telehealth would allow them to see patients. The embrace of telehealth by providers was unbelievable. So, today our business is much more diverse.

We still have a significant command over the payer side, where we run most of the national payers, most of the Blue Cross Blue Shields, and so on. But we have about half of our business with the provider side, where we run different kinds of telehealth for health systems, and we have growth in government business as well. But it took a while to get here.

And now we also have accounts overseas. We acquired a couple of companies that have international penetration in other geographic areas, so we're out there. But at the beginning, it was American. The company was founded in Delaware as American Well, and it became Amwell because people just started shortening the name. It kind of made sense, and Amwell hasn't been a problem name overseas, funny enough. So, we're good there.

Regarding competitors, Teladoc was a company for a couple of years before we showed up. They had a different model than our model for about 15 years, as Teladoc offered audio interaction with the patient over the telephone. On the other hand, we were always making sure that the patient and the clinician could *see each other* to meet the needs of the medical boards and what they considered to be the threshold of good care at that time. Seeing the patient and seeing the doctor became very, very important. We battled for, I don't know, maybe ten years around the video aspect, and then eventually, Teladoc started doing video, and we became very similar.

However, I would say that there are two other distinctions between the two companies that are probably still true. One is that Teladoc, for the most part, chose to work with employers as their target market. We have always believed that the payers and the clinicians, the health plans and the clinicians, are the ones who are going to promote Amwell. I don't want to speak for Teladoc; I think they're a great company doing many things right in many ways. But they always believed that the way to do it is to have their clients direct patients to Teladoc, which became a brand. And people would go to Teladoc, whereas, to this day, we have the "Intel Inside"[3] model. 99.9% of the people who use Amwell have no idea that they're using Amwell. When they use our product, the patients see their Blue Cross Blue Shield logo, or they're seeing their hospital logo, or they're seeing the logo of another organization that was giving them a benefit, or their employer's brand. In short, we're under the hood, actually running it for them, and as you can imagine, this is a very different go-to-market strategy. It's also a very different technology and a very different architecture because we don't think that we're the story. We're a cog in the wheel, and I think that has helped us a lot over the years.

> ***They are still the largest out there, but to scale you need two different things. One is, you need to be able to reach down the market from the aircraft carriers to the regional operators and so on. And two, you need to begin to think about how you guarantee, that as more and more organizations come in, that you can handle the volume of service providers – not only the technology.***

The moment we started scaling was very important because the original funding – that quick Series A – was quite substantial. If I recall correctly, I think it was like $50 million or something that we brought to start the company. And that was 17 years ago, so quite a lot of money. But we needed that type of investment because we knew that we needed to change the mindset of the industry, to have the industry do something that hadn't been done before. The initial build-out of the product and its initial rollouts were proving grounds that you could distribute healthcare over technology. Those initial partners were very valuable because, to this day, they are the movers and shakers of the industry. That hasn't changed. They are still the largest out there, but to scale, you need two different things. One is, you need to be able to reach down the market from the aircraft carriers to the regional operators and so on. And two, you need to begin to think about how you guarantee that, as more and more organizations come in, that you can handle the volume of service providers – not only the technology. At the end of the day, we're a switchboard, right? So that was when we did another significant funding round.

It was all about scaling and the understanding that we needed to develop both the technology and build our own network of clinicians all over the country, in all 50 states. It must be 24/7, load balanced, highly trained, and highly quality controlled – and that's a big build–out. That's when the second tranche of funding came in.

Technology was different then, too. There was no cloud. The only clouds were in the sky when it was windy. There was a lot of apprehension by everybody that something extremely private, like getting your healthcare, was going to be done using technology. However, it also helped that, unlike the Teladoc model, we were not the front brand. So, if you trusted your Blue Cross Blue Shield, Intermountain Healthcare, Stanford Health, Ochsner, or any one of those customers that we have, then getting the services from them through technology was fine. And it was especially helpful when you needed it right now or your kids needed it right now. Later, we added behavioral health. And when you had a desperate need, this technology was very much a lifesaver.

And then, we made a point of really encouraging people to tell their story. Good and bad. We weren't moderating it. We said, "Our purpose is to give people another option when healthcare is otherwise unavailable to them." And we walked the walk. I think it resonated with a subset of the population. There were always people who said no. Some were the business makers who said no, or the couple of regulators who said no, or patients who said, "I will never do this." And there were physicians and clinicians who also said no, but you don't have to persuade everybody. It's not your job. I'm just happy that the critical mass was enough to give Amwell a life of its own.

It's not unlike what's going on with AI now. I mean, the story rewrites itself. We're going to have tremendous capabilities in AI to help with our healthcare, with knowledge, with guidance, with reassurance, with navigational help, and everything else. There are going to be people who accept it and there are going to be people who strongly oppose it. And there are going to be some bad apples and some mistakes along the way. Some people will get hurt, but that doesn't mean that the technology is all bad. We just need to make it better.

Before the cloud, we had our own data centers, and they were certified by our clients. Our solution ran from our data centers as a white–labeled solution that was tied into their systems. But then we had to transition to the cloud, which was less complicated in some ways, like scalability. Technological scalability becomes, both vertically and horizontally, much easier in the cloud. On the flip side, you don't control everything, and clouds do have issues. I want to say for the record, services go down, and you are obligated by your SLAs [service level agreements] to your customers, and they don't care if there was an AWS shutdown or Google Cloud shutdown. (We use both.)

The transition to the cloud became apparent to us when scaling became a requirement, not a novelty. And that was during COVID-19. We had our systems; the original product that was developed all these years ago actually worked pretty well all the way up to COVID-19. It had evolved over the years and had continually improved. But the client-server, on-prem model worked fine, and then during COVID-19, all hell broke loose. We also happened to take the company public during COVID-19 – honest to God, we didn't intend for it to happen that way. Taking a company public is a three-year exercise, so we started long before COVID-19, but then COVID-19 showed up. We took the company public during COVID-19, and we had a very, very good initial public offering (IPO), which gave us the capability to say, "We now have a radically different understanding of the role of these technologies in healthcare." There was no way we could patch our old systems to do what the new world of telehealth would require. So, we decided to bite the bullet and create it all over again from scratch.

> ***We literally built a shadow software company inside Amwell that was isolated and dedicated to building a whole new world of telehealth 15 years after the legacy systems were built.***

We literally built a shadow software company inside Amwell that was isolated and dedicated to building a whole new world of telehealth 15 years after the legacy systems were built. Frankly, I can tell you, I can't imagine where we would be if we didn't make that decision. We have truly amazing technology today, but we paid a price, especially when you look at the burn rate, the number of resources we had to consume in order to essentially run a second software company under the budget of another software company. It's something that a lot of people have real trouble with because the cash burn is huge. Luckily, this is now behind us. These new systems are up and running in the environment and are doing amazingly well. So, things are normalizing.

As for the IPO, I don't know if there is one thing that led us to an IPO. First, not only for the investors in the company and the shareholders but also for employees and others, taking a company public is validation on many, many levels. It establishes you as a more credible organization. It gives you the resources, the wings, to do extremely bold things like major acquisitions or re-platforming, which is not for the faint of heart. It's also a process that forces certain maturation of all the company's operations and leadership. It gives a whole new meaning to the term "accountability." And it was time for that to happen.

I think that because most of Amwell's customers are relatively large organizations at the national level or very large regionals, it became apparent that telehealth was becoming more and more strategic to them. It was no longer an innovation thing but rather part of the way they do business, and they wanted it to have that kind of credibility.

> ***And in healthcare, building credibility is something that takes a very long time, and establishing ourselves as a public company with that caliber of customers was a natural thing for us to do.***

Years ago, the saying was, "Nobody got fired for choosing IBM," right? I don't know about today, but it mattered then. And in healthcare, building credibility is something that takes a very long time, and establishing ourselves as a public company with that caliber of customers was a natural thing for us to do. We were also very fortunate, in a way, that COVID-19 happened and took people's understanding of what these technologies could do to a whole other level. We would not have been able to do one-tenth of what we do today with our legacy platforms if we hadn't invested in re-platforming. If a company hasn't gone public, making the decision to spend $400–500 million on building another platform, on top of the one they already have, is inconceivable.

> ***But the decision to work alongside others and understand that we were only going to be successful if we made our customers successful – our success was through them – was one of the best decisions we made.***

Additionally, there were a few pivotal decisions that were very important and led us to the scale we have now. The first one probably was the decision to work with partners and not go direct [to consumers]. This is tough because we wanted to go to employers and direct to consumer (DTC). We strongly believed that our solution delivered value directly to people, so why not go DTC? But the healthcare industry humbles you. Healthcare operates very differently from any other business. And I can talk a lot about that. But the decision to work alongside others and understand that we were only going to be successful if we made our customers successful – our success was through them – was one of the best decisions we made. That said, this was something that we questioned ourselves repeatedly for years.

I think the second very important decision we made was to stick with video, because there was a time when telehealth was phone or video, and video is much harder to do. No question about it. Because the clinicians needed to be on camera, they needed to have a webcam, which not everyone had. There was no iPhone at the beginning, so it was very complicated technology. But we believed that people wanted to *see* a doctor, and that meant something to us. And so, we built our entire operation around the notion that this sentiment is critical. It also allowed us to work gradually, getting the medical boards to feel comfortable with it and getting the large payers involved in it. So that was another good decision we made.

Frankly, the third decision was to build the Amwell Converge™ platform[4] [Amwell's hybrid solution] to understand that those old technologies that give you the application that allows you to see a doctor are missing out on the new world of telehealth, which is logistics. It isn't about the video conferencing anymore. Allowing healthcare to be redistributed over technology and the logistics behind it is a whole different ball game than having a video app – I'll tell you that. So that decision to build Converge, which is our new platform, thank God, was a good one.

> ***[W]e successfully became partners with many of the organizations that we serve. And I can't emphasize how important that is, especially in this business.***

Looking forward, if we put aside the stock market behavior, which is a whole other fun area with the ebb and flow, we're extremely well capitalized. We don't need to raise capital anytime soon, but it will continue to ebb and flow. We have a lot of business in the market, and we have successfully become partners with many of the organizations that we serve. And I can't emphasize how important that is, especially in this business. But I think, frankly, this is more technology than just healthcare. It moves way faster than other healthcare businesses because it is associated with interactive experiences. People do Instagram and TikTok and all that kind of stuff. That's the way they expect interactions to happen. Immediate gratification. Entitlement and everything. These are very real, and they usually don't exist in healthcare. Usually, we go and sit and wait for an hour until someone is ready to see us. Then we sit again, and we're asked, "Do you have any questions?" We say no because you don't want to take anybody's time. That world is very different. What has happened over the last couple of years is that people have accepted that some of their healthcare will happen through technology. That is way more profound than just telehealth. It means that technology can become a companion for people who need regular companionship – people who are suffering every day. I'm not talking about the people who go to urgent care because they have the flu, but people who have cancer, or are elderly, or have chronic conditions, and people who are teetering at their own home before they need to go to a skilled nursing facility, and their families, and so on. Technology can become an always-on companion to people in those very challenging parts of their lives. It's not going to be just seeing a doctor. It's going to be there always with the ability to bring in a clinician if the situation commands it. That partnership will allow us to dramatically change, on the one hand, our experience with healthcare as people, and on the other hand, the way that we can, as a country, afford healthcare because it will move a lot of healthcare services to the patient's environment, which is where everybody wants to be – and is the lowest-cost care setting.

That is what's upon us, and what that means is that we need to morph. We need to change fast, and again. We need to accept the notion that automated, always-on interaction with patients is real. You need to do it right. AI is real, and it needs to be supportive of your relationship with clinicians rather than replacing your relationship with clinicians. And AI is going to change every nook and cranny of what we call healthcare. We're in a good position to do it because we are already technologically present for many, many millions of people who are using us for traditional telehealth.

Becoming a Unicorn, or whatever you call it, is an empowering position because you can do much more. And that's it. That's the only thing we thought. I mean, we were happy for shareholders, employees, and colleagues who worked very hard and believed in our mission. But what we really thought about was, "OK, now what?" Maybe it's a personality thing. I'm not sure it's the same for everybody, but that was my experience with it.

As for establishing this and other companies with my brother [Ido[5]], the first consideration is that you don't go away. You don't part ways, right? That's not going to happen. And if you care about your family, and I do care about my family very much, it means that you need to constantly be aware, on the one hand, not only of what you like to do but also of what your family member wants to do, and of what you're good at and what he is good at. That's also changing over time, so you need to constantly revisit that balance. You need to actively invest in maintaining that balance, as it's not something that happens naturally. I think we were lucky that my heart and passion are in technology, product, and disruptive innovation. And while I was disrupting to some degree, he was always the guy who liked investor relations, business development, sales, and that kind of stuff. So, it really worked well for three companies now. But I can tell you, you also must ask yourself, what is healthy for the partnership? When do you part ways? Because you can find passions in different ways. It needs to be there only when it's constructive and positive. We were very lucky. Normally, people would say, "Don't mix family with business" or "Don't mix friends with business." If it happens naturally, then let it be, but don't force it.

Going broader, we have had so many opportunities as a country to understand that if we pull together, we're better off. And not just this country. In fact, many small groups of people realize that if you pull together, you're better off. And yet the business of healthcare isn't pulling together. It is separated in so many ways. Different people with different interests, different states with different licensure requirements, different insurance models, and the practice of medicine differ from one place to another. So, we haven't had the leadership we need. Maybe Washington? Maybe that's where it needs to be, at the federal level, to rethink how people experience healthcare now that technology allows us to pull together. I live in Boston, and every other building here is a hospital. I can see any specialist I want, but drive out west and access takes a nosedive. It disappears. There's no reason why an oncologist from Dana-Farber or Memorial Sloan Kettering, who knows the best protocols to treat a certain kind of cancer, shouldn't be available to a primary care physician in West Texas to help them care for a patient there. We don't do this because of financial reasons, which is how the world works, but also because of ego and muscle memory. We must grow up. And I hope that we will have leaders who will walk in and say enough is enough. Let's figure out how to safely do this, because without healthcare, life is very painful.

All that said, I love what I do. It's nice to be part of a group of people that will change the world.

2.5 Notes

Endnotes

1 https://business.amwell.com/about-us
2 https://my.pitchbook.com/profile/57380-68/company/profile#insights
3 https://www.intel.com/content/www/us/en/history/virtual-vault/articles/end-user-marketing-intel-inside.html
4 https://business.amwell.com/converge-hybrid-care-platform
5 https://www.linkedin.com/in/ido-schoenberg-80711779/

Chapter 3

athenahealth

It was a combination of agile discovery of whether what we were doing was too complicated or not, agile discovery of whether it was too hard or not, and raw luck.

–Jonathan Bush, Co-founder

3.1 Quick Facts

Website	https://www.athenahealth.com/
Founded	1997
Mission	*Providing care can be simpler* *Make achieving your best possible outcomes easier with athenaOne, our all-in-one healthcare solution that enables clinical and operational efficiency.*[1]
Founders[2]	Jonathan Bush https://www.linkedin.com/in/jonathanbushjr/ Todd Park https://www.linkedin.com/in/todd-park-3232573/
Unicorn status achieved	2015
Funding rounds[3]	30 funding deals • October 1997–June 2024 (IPO in 2007) • Range from $2.6 million to $294 million (Buyout)

DOI: 10.4324/9781032711034-3

Notable funders	• GGV Capital • Oak Investment Partners • Eastside Partners • Lambda Funds • Undisclosed Angel Investors

3.2 TLDR

Ideate

- Founded by Jonathan Bush and Todd Park
- Initial focus on maternity care, later shifted to technology
- Aim to simplify healthcare and improve outcomes with athenaOne
- Unicorn status achieved in 2015
- Notable funders include GGV Capital, Oak Investment Partners, and Lambda Funds

Build

- Developed a billing system for maternity care clinics
- Created athenaNet, a website for screening Medicaid coverage
- Focus on solving complex problems in healthcare billing
- Transitioned from maternity care to billing solutions
- Built a cloud-based infrastructure for healthcare providers

Launch

- Worked with smaller clinics and hospitals to implement athenaNet
- Expanded customer base through acquisitions by for-profit hospitals
- Added functionalities like patient communications and night call services
- Launched electronic medical records (EMR) system
- IPO with $100 million in revenue

Grow

- Hosted company TV shows and all-hands meetings to maintain corporate culture
- Created the Schein tree to map corporate culture
- Expanded product offerings and customer base
- Raised multiple funding rounds, including mezzanine and IPO
- Continued innovation and adaptation to market changes

3.3 Meet the Founder

Jonathan Bush

Jonathan Bush is currently the founder and CEO of Zus Health, a company building the first shared health data platform designed to accelerate healthcare data interoperability by providing easy-to-use patient data at the point of care.

Mr. Bush also sits on the board of Innovaccer, a company building a series of technology platform services for population health. He is the co-founder and former CEO of athenahealth, one of the earliest cloud-based billing and EMR platforms that now serves over 20 percent of the US market, and former executive chairman of Firefly Health, a pioneer in real-time virtual primary care.

Prior to founding athenahealth, Mr. Bush served as an emergency medical technician for the City of New Orleans, was trained as a medic in the US Army, and worked as a management consultant with Booz Allen & Hamilton. Mr. Bush obtained a Bachelor of Arts in the College of Social Studies from Wesleyan University and an MBA. from Harvard Business School and currently lives in Cape Elizabeth, Maine, with his family.

3.4 Interview with Jonathan Bush, CEO and Co-founder

athenahealth started as a women's clinic but then moved to more of a technology-focused company. We've all seen companies that operate along this continuum trying to find the right spot for themselves in the ecosystem. But if there's a clear customer need that's already been identified, there are too many people already doing it with more money, skill, and ability than your frail little startup.

> ***You must get the customer's need just right, just beyond their view, but not so far out of view that they think you are a lunatic.***

If your idea and company are too complicated, you're just a raving lunatic, and no one buys what you are trying to sell. You must get the customer's need just right, just beyond their view, but not so far out of view that they think you are a lunatic.

Another major issue is the complexity of the build. It's got to be something that's hard enough to build that they'll let you suck at it for a while, compared to doing it themselves, but it can't be so hard to build that you crash the bus before you get started.

> ***I went right to building something that was unbelievably complicated to build.***

In my case, I went all the way because I was fearful of not being unique enough. I went right to building something that was unbelievably complicated to build. Part of the complexity was that it was unbelievably hard for people to understand and articulate what they wanted: to completely redo maternity care in a way that actually threatened the established OBGYN ecosystem.

I said to the doubters,

> ***If you're one of the ones who do this first, you're going to dramatically improve the quality, cost, and customer satisfaction, without doing all the things you used to do. As the manager of 10 midwives, you're going to make more money treating sicker people and you'll be more satisfied.***

But it was a long stretch for them to believe in the vision.

Similarly, there were several things we had to get right, Todd and I, and our little band of idealists. This meant we had to completely redo the service experience, convincing doctors that they wanted to co-practice with midwives rather than just make the decision themselves. We had to convince the insurance companies to pay us for creating savings when we had no money to guarantee it on our balance sheet.

> ***All we had was a ream of very hard solves to do and we sort of drove with all our might to make it happen.***

All we had was a ream of very hard solves to do and we sort of drove with all our might to make it happen. Oh, and throw in one more continuum: where are you in the good luck spectrum? Is the wind about to hit your behind, or is the wind about to hit you in the face? Managed care was peaking in the late 1990s and about to turn, and we were about to go anti-managed care for a period of time. Everyone was thinking, "Ohh!

California's capitation model is coming east." California was covering people for $150 per member per month, but people were complaining, waiting in line, and being told where to go to get care.

Then we had the Internet boom, and Clinton essentially said, "I'm not going to piss everybody off." So, we had the "it's too complicated, too hard to understand value" wind turning into our faces. Luckily, we started dying slowly by paddling very hard upwind on all these fronts, but we didn't completely disappear. We slowly faded, and as we did, we realized that inside this incredibly hard-to-deliver thing is billing – just knowing whether the person is even covered. Among many of the things we were doing to pull together this complicated build, we had built a little website that could screen scrape the state Medicaid in California (Medi-Cal) provider and tell you the status of a patient and whether they were covered this month. Once you get a job, you're not covered anymore. You're out. Lose your job, and you get back in. It's highly dynamic.

If they are using a midwife, there is a certain modifier that needs to be part of your claim that no one understands. There were all these little, idiosyncratic things that we had built into this website that all the lovely ladies at our clinic reception desks could use. But that was just one of the 1,000 projects going on.

And then the tectonic plates began shifting; the winds were continuing, and all these HMOs were merging. Their claims systems were being combined and iterated, and doctors had no idea where to send their claims or how to get them paid.

While managed care was kind of on the "outs," getting paid and figuring out claims was on the "ins." San Diego County happened to be the first county running this experiment with SAIC on a new thing called digital service language, which could run a digital signal over a copper wire. Who knew? It was a complete accident, but we could have our little midwife clinics using high-speed(ish) Internet for $42 a month.

So, the timing and wind changed from our face to our rear. And in terms of understanding the problem again, doctors weren't eager to be told that they were doing it wrong and they should practice with midwives and become more communal in their care. But they sure were dying for someone to take over these horrible claims, baloney. For us, this was the shift, which was all three of those got better.

I was desperately trying to find one more investor who would fund us in this "too complicated, too hard to understand," wind in our face idea . . .

We would have missed it, but as I was desperately trying to find one more investor who would fund us in this "too complicated, too hard to understand," wind-in-our-face idea, I met this guy who was managing money for a venture capitalist. He was managing money for an oilman and was planning to set up a capital fund and family office so the investor could diversify from oil. One of his areas of interest was healthcare.

He and I are sitting in the birthing room with the glider rocking chairs, and I'm trying to get him to experience how important it would be to invest. His response was,

> *Listen, I just don't think you can get the doctors to do all this. And you have too many people and too many things going on. I don't want to invest, but I'll give you $11 million for that website (that we called athenaNet). If you give me unlimited license to use athenaNet, I'll get it and then you can use it to build your birthing centers and prove me wrong. You can be my customer and I'll be your software vendor.*

And I'm like, really?

> *We* were *doing way too much.*

I went back to Todd and said, "The good news is, I think we're going to live. The bad news is all the midwives are fired." We *were* doing way too much. It was a very painful emotional transition because the clinics and midwives were how we started. It was a combination of agile discovery of whether what we were doing was too complicated or not, agile discovery of whether it was too hard or not, and raw luck.

Like a lot of companies, as I was describing it, our solution was an internal tool. It was an enabler, so we were the first customers of this product. And so the product feedback cycle was very fast.

In contrast, in my current startup, Zus [https://zushealth.com], we announced our financing with these three huge-name customers, and everyone was so excited, the valuation was through the roof. We could never get a meeting with our customers. They had a few vague ideas, but they didn't really want to waste a lot of time with us. Whereas the guys who built Slack – it was their internal system because they were trying to build a video game. And at athena, we were like that. We were trying to build a birthing center, and we ended up with a billing system for the birthing center, or actually a set of systems related to billing. We had already taken it through many, many iterations by the time we showed it to the first customer. Our first customer was deciding between death and dishonor, as that customer had been part of a staff model HMO where they had never had to bill. It was all just covered, like Kaiser, and they had been fired.

This staff model HMO was giving up the staff model part and just being an HMO, and so they were either going to close or start paying rent on their office building. We found them through another miraculous friend of a friend and told the HMO that we would stand up everything. We will do all of it. We'll put it in your computers. We'll attach them to printers. We will train your staff. We did a terrible job, but we did a much better job than they just closing. And we wouldn't have been able to even do that if we hadn't been eating our own dog food for three years before that.

At the time, the healthcare billing systems world was dominated by on-premise servers. You would buy a minicomputer and put it in your basement, refrigerate it, and then drag wires around your office. Remember those Cat-5 cables that would click when you inserted them into a computer? IDX systems [a large healthcare technology company acquired by GE Healthcare[4]] were big in larger practices, and Cerner was the big one for hospitals. But there were others, too, like HBO & Co. and McKesson [who eventually bought HBO & Co.[5]]. There was a whole litany of these hospital systems and doctor systems that were traditional software – you buy a disk from them, they send it to you; you buy servers, some guy comes and sticks something in them.

> ***[T]here were no electronic medical records.***

One of the reasons we built athenaNet was that we did not have the money to buy any of those systems at that stage. We had only raised $1.6 million, and there was no interoperability; there were no electronic medical records (EMRs). Most of the systems were stay management systems (they called them ADT systems, Admission, Discharge, Transfer systems) or billing systems. On the ambulatory side, they had Practice Management Information Systems, again for managing the logistics of the visit in Room 1 (ready for doctor, ready for checkout, checkout), and the machine would take the data, turn them into claims, and push them to a printer or to a claims intermediary for further processing.

We were in a landscape where there was no such thing as an Internet-native system.

There were a few companies that said, "Look, you don't want to buy one of these systems. We've bought one. We'll set up terminals at your office, or we'll drive the paper from your office to our terminals." And we said, "[T]hat's our model" because we had already said to our first set of customers, "Make us a 20% partner in the profits." We already had the idea that we were on the same side as the doctor [there were no upfront costs]. Now, we told customers, "Make us a 5% partner in the revenues," which honestly wasn't that different. Additionally, we said, "We'll only get paid when you get paid." That way it'll be on us to get everything – all the capital investments of systems and servers will be on us. Little did they know we weren't going to get any servers. We're going to just use the Internet.

> ***We were lucky to be growing up in a time when there were many, many, many private practices – hundreds of thousands of them around the country.***

We were lucky to be growing up in a time when there were many, many, many private practices – hundreds of thousands of them around the country. (This was before the Obama-era roll-up, where every practice got acquired by a hospital. Today, more than 80% of doctors work for a hospital, and about half of them are miserable working for the hospital. We may see a reversal of this trend.) At the time, 80% of doctors worked for themselves in little tribes. And the key issues within those practices were things like:

- Which partner's spouse would get to be the CFO of the practice?
- Who's putting more hours in on admin?
- Who should still be let in if they did more surgeries?

These practices of typically eight doctors ended up dealing with tribal types of politics. Practices larger than eight would need to be brave enough to get a real CEO to take them all the way to 40, which were the big practices, with few exceptions. There were enough practices, such that we could find the fools who didn't know we were a nobody. It was a frog-kissing endeavor.

Let's go back to the example of the HMO group that had just been fired. They didn't have the money to buy any of these systems. And then as we got a few doctors who became references, they would tell their friends. A reference from a friend, in that tribal world, was gold. You must make the golf game, as we used to say.

US Airways would make the golf game because they would make everybody motion sick and wait and lose their drinks. "Oh! You wouldn't believe my flight!" But could you make the golf game a positive experience? We wanted customers to say,

> *Oh my God, I can't believe it. You know I got 20% more money than I thought using this internet thing where they do it for you. I don't understand it, but it's called athene. Have you heard of athene?*

And that was how we got from one to 40 customers.

> ***We also bumped into universal low-cost, high-speed internet in the first city.***

We also bumped into universal low-cost, high-speed Internet in the first city. And we were starting to spread nationally at the same time. For years, we had a department of Internet access that oversaw trying to find Internet at different addresses. Often it wouldn't be there, and we would have to rent an A-frame relay circuit to a place where there was, and then it would be an extra $100 a month or whatever. And then we would have to convince the customer that it was worth the extra expense.

Also, my cofounder Todd's [Park] younger brother, Ed "Eddie" Park, was president of the Harvard Computer Club and was kind of the desktop support mafia for the undergrads at Harvard. We convinced him to spend summers with us, showing him what we were starting with, and he's like, "This is terrible!" And my founding CTO [Todd] was also watching the Internet and thinking to himself, "This stuff isn't that hard. We could build this." We found a local entrepreneur in San Diego who offered to underwrite the building of the system if we would lend him Bob Gatewood and Eddie.

And then our entrepreneur friend went bust, and all of Bob and Eddie's work was our hostage. We took Bob and Eddie's work back and stood it up in a server in one of our apartments connected to the Internet. And we kept going, with Todd as chief software architect, CTO, and president. (Todd is now CEO of Devoted Health. (https://www.devoted.com/).) Todd is probably the only CEO of a major company in America who writes code every night and releases it into production.

We were just unbelievably fortunate to have people who were like that. It was Perl script, which is a scripting language that was just out, making it easier to write very bad software quickly. We built macros in the early days of the Apple suite. And so, we just had string upon string upon string of macros that did these little jobs. One of the many reasons I was fired is I had never refactored that. By the time I was doing it, it was costing too much and not going well enough. We had maybe 45 million lines of squirrel string at the time it was sold.

But stepping back, we had worked with several smaller clinics in the 40-doctor range. Kaiser launched in Massachusetts at one point and failed, and fired all the doctors. We found them there, all huddled in a circle with their Birkenstocks and their socialist medicine manuals. They had hoped to continue the way they operated, but in a fee-for-service world it wouldn't work. We said, "We'll take it off your hands. You won't have to worry about it." I think they were customer number eight or something like that, and they are still a customer. It went that way for quite a while.

Some of those groups were acquired by their local hospitals, and suddenly, we either were fired or made the platform. When a hospital is going on an acquisition spree, the idea of no CapEx, no hiring, and an implementation that takes weeks, not months or years, becomes very appealing.

The real enterprise play was when a series of for-profit hospitals, most of them based in Nashville, TN, and very capital conscious, said,

> *Holy Moses, this is great! I can buy a practice and in four weeks have them live in a single nerve center. I can see every stroke of work in their practice and change protocols. This company is changing all the intelligence underneath it.*

Because we built the solution for ourselves, when we built another tablespace[6] for another customer that wasn't us, we used the same insurance list that we had built for ourselves for them. Now we weren't just selling software and work – we were selling *knowledge*. We were selling answers. And attached to those insurance lists, that one single national insurance list, were all the claim adjudication rules that we had learned about over time.

Each new copy of athena was just a tablespace inside of one big system. Anytime a claim was denied by anyone for any customer, we figured out the root cause, asking the five whys.[7] If we could build a rule based on what we learned, nobody would ever get that claim denied again anywhere, even people who never met each other. There was a giant network effect. The nice thing about these corporate accounts was that they understood the real value of what they had, and they began to use it aggressively to make acquisitions. That became a real lift for us, both in terms of credibility, but also those were sales that we never had to close. They would just buy practices hand over fist, and our revenues would go up as they brought on the new practices.

> ***We were riding the acquisition wave and the cloud technology wave.***

We were riding the acquisition wave and the cloud technology wave. And then every couple of years, we would add a job to do, like patient communications. One scenario was people weren't showing up for appointments that were in the providers' calendar; maybe we should send them a reminder text message. So, we bought the company that does that.

Another was night call, when patients call their doctor's answering service. The answering service has no idea who you are because they can't see anything. What if we offered that information embedded into the system? Then, of course, there were the medical records. The topic of medical records was a bugaboo because it was a forced march with the HITECH Act,[8] and the federal government specified the features that met the definition of an electronic health record. And they were bad features. I mean well-meaning, non-corrupt people doing their best in a rush to get their moment in the sun. And it was not federated, so there was no logical equivalent of the insurance list. Each customer had to be a separate provider's list.

Separate patient list. Separate chart list. All of which was crazy, because the patient showed up in all these different places. Much of the reason I'm still working is I'd like to see that change. Still today, there are no medical record systems of any kind that federate data across customers, which is absolutely weird.

> ***Then we had this huge one, which was the electronic medical record, which we had to do, as it was a make-or-break job for us.***

We would add a new job to do, try it, and as soon as it was working, we would try another. Often the ones we tried would not work so we would scrap that one and try another one. Then we had this huge one, which was the electronic medical record, which we had to do, as it was a make-or-break job for us.

Providers were all required to get on an electronic medical record or some other system that had an EMR in it. We were going to either get a share of this market or lose it. We had a big lift to make this happen. We did better than most, but we did not elect to build out [all the workflows of] the whole hospital. Our larger thesis was that people needed to get more care outside of the hospital than in. The HITECH Act had the unintended consequence of moving physician ownership and a lot of care to higher-cost settings. We did fine, but it didn't strengthen our strategic position as much as I think a more agile, natural approach would have.

When building a company, a lot of companies sort of drag along, drag along, drag along, always planning to do better than they do, always planning to do better than they do. When suddenly, something happens and they start to do better than they planned, better than they planned, better than they planned. Then they start getting used to that [level of success], and they think, "Oh yeah, no problem." They don't realize that if they click that model and drag it to the right, they are going to be bigger than Russia in 20 years because of the law of large numbers. And then they start to do worse than they planned, worse than they planned. Great CEOs look ahead so that you have the infrastructure, governance, bureaucracy, overhead, and processes you need for where the ball's *going to be* because it takes a while to pivot.

> ***At athenahealth, we loved the idea of pretending to be a big company, pretending to have the process and the governance in place.***

At athenahealth, we loved the idea of pretending to be a big company, pretending to have the process and the governance in place. We even called my secondhand Grand Wagoneer with a broken window the Athena One, like it was our corporate jet. And we would take Athena One to Walden Pond for picnics. We'd all climb into the back of Athena One. Then there was a day when there were two of them [Wagoneers], purchased at the right time, when they actually made money for the company and were useful to the company. That idea of playing house, but in a corporate sense, operating like the company we *wanted* to be, served us very well for a very long time. And I think playing house, or this tongue-in-cheek treatment of it, as opposed to taking it too seriously, also served us well for a long time.

Eventually, our growth flattened out. I ran the company for 22 years, and the last year I was there, we grew 21% organically from a billion dollars. So, we weren't failing, but we also didn't sustain 30% growth. We had spent a lot to get there, and we weren't putting up the requisite profit. I spoke with our investors all the time, and they never said they cared, even though I should have known that they cared. They kept saying, "You are doing fine;

keep going." But when an activist came in and said, "Look at all the money he wastes," I couldn't say no. I proudly spent the money for the purpose of continuing to try to capture this moment in time, with all the macro forces at play. So, I think playing house in the beginning allows people to take things seriously without becoming too political. They can try out more mature ways of operating without taking themselves too seriously and without sticky bureaucracy if they get it wrong.

We always tried to live and operate like we would need to a year or two hence.

We always tried to live and operate like we would need to a year or two hence. And by the time that year or two had passed, we were actually able to do it easily. But when I was trying to get people to do new things, it was more like playing house. Let's just try it, doing it for the fun of it; I made fun of it and made sure everyone else made fun of it, too.

This not-taking-things-too-seriously was used whether we were building campuses that were thematically consistent and had this notion of a national backbone (which is what we wanted to be, the nation's health information backbone) or whether it was making sure that I had an in-person schedule that would hold the office together. We made sure that we added offices, each with its own Michael Porter competitive advantage based on its geography,[9] and that we got it early enough that we didn't hire people with that competitive advantage in the wrong place and then force them to move. Of course, all these things that go away with Zoom life were a big deal then.

We'd host a Squawk Box type of company TV show, like a news show, and then also host all-hands quarterly meetings styled after the Johnny Carson Show. These were important to impart the corporate culture.

We also wanted to make sure that people still felt close as the crowd got bigger. We'd host a Squawk Box type of company TV show, like a news show, and then also host all-hands quarterly meetings styled after the Johnny Carson Show. These were important to impart the corporate culture. Most people would call this culture management, but I feel like it's more culture chasing or culture herding. You can't really manage culture, but you can play ball with it. You can get in there and tussle with it. The most powerful thing you can do is name where your culture is, whether or not it is where you want it to be. That actually shapes the culture more than most things. And then you can say, "I'm trying this thing to change our underlying culture." To me, the underlying assumption is that you don't say it out loud – about how to get ahead at work. You know good shit happens and bad shit happens. Then you have what management says, what management does in the office, and what happens in the world. A cocktail of those three things shaken together to form those underlying assumptions.

We had this idea to create the Schein tree, based on the work of Edgar Schein, who wrote the theory of cultural leadership at MIT.[10] He never created a tree, but he talked about artifacts that you see in the office relating to policies that drive the underlying assumptions. The combination of the things you see, the policies, and the management practices all feed the roots of a corporate culture. We would build a tree every year, and we would say, "Do people see things in the office that makes them think, 'Oh, I'm Athena'?" One year we got to a size where everybody had to wear ID tags, and our first thought was, how can we make this not a bureaucratic bullshit thing but something that we were proud of and really used? It was an artifact. Policies had to be followed because we were SOC2 certified[11] and needed to focus on security.

We asked our teams what our underlying assumptions were: we're growing up; we're bureaucratic. We let people map the routes they thought we had said. We learned what policies people were talking about and what artifacts made people feel like they were at athena. And that was very helpful for bringing people together. It was far enough away from the brutal work of building a business but related enough that it was the right sort of psychic distance from quarterly planning that people could be themselves, fall out of character, and be vulnerable, yet still be relevant in the workplace. I spent an enormous amount of time on that kind of thing. As the leader, it was important to set the tone for the company, even if you didn't want to. I think you can set a good tone if you're lucky, and I was happy with our tone most of the way.

We had one period when we had a CFO who couldn't change management information systems, leading to a period of time when we had to use our judgment instead of data. We were used to having unbelievable data because we had every click of every user all the way up. But without the data, we created a culture where whoever was loudest in a meeting or the pushiest one won, because there was no data to use for a while. You could see the consequences of that just ripple through the business during that transition.

Our first round of funding started with my mom and dad and aunts and uncles and every former boss from Booz Allen.

Our first round of funding started with my mom and dad and aunts and uncles and every former boss from Booz Allen. The cost was $50,000 a unit. A couple of people took two units; one guy took four units. The investors were like, "Why not watch John Bush's son and this friend of his, see what they can do." Then we went back to them because we needed some more, and about half of them came back. At this point, we had $900,000, and we realized we needed to figure it out by the time we needed more. And we realized that we weren't going to get there, then we had this billing idea.

So, we reshaped the company and then went to professional funders and venture capitalists, and we were able to get a grizzled, old VC to say he was in, and that made the other VCs pounce. We valued the company at, I think, $11 million – literally the $11 million that the guy valued the company for the software. And we were able to raise $11 million. We gave away half the company to these VCs, and we thought, OK, now we've got more money than we will ever, ever need. We are the Federal Reserve.

We have $11 million.

We started doing free company lunches at the local Cambodian place. We started getting those [Aeron] chairs with the fancy buttons everywhere, and then we realized, whoa, whoa, whoa. We had to pull back. We started really getting into the microeconomics of making it work. We did get a few of those for-profit hospital players and one nonprofit that was very avaricious, Baylor in Dallas. And that gave us room to raise a mezzanine round with those names and our novel concept. We had raised money as an Internet play, and none of the people that we had pitched the birthing center play touched it with a 10-foot pole because they were thinking, "You're just desperate. You're making shit up. You know you don't know anything about the internet." All of which was true.

Interestingly, I got a huge gift from this guy who was one of the Angel Investors, a classmate of mine from business school. He said,

> *You know, I've invested in every guy in our section, and who asked me. Every single one of them, if it didn't work perfectly the first time,*

> *crashed the business, took the idea, and started again with a new cap table. You didn't. You kept your birthing center people in your internet billing play, which you know, is 1/10th of the business.*

But you know, they didn't know what they were investing in. Eventually, we did end up with a very small slice of athena, Todd and I. It never bothered us, even for a minute, until the day we were fired by the activists. Then it bothered me a lot, but until then, it didn't bother me.

> ***That idea of earning the right to get to the next level and having a few key milestones – that's important.***

That idea of earning the right to get to the next level and having a few key milestones – that's important. Once that second mezzanine investor came in, I think the VCs actually thought they had something, and they convinced me to do another follow-on round, mostly for their partner funds. It was money that I did not need. I made up a really big number. I remember sitting on the toilet on my cell phone thinking, this is a really big number that will make them leave us alone. Before I got off the toilet, they said yes! And I'm thinking, oh shit! I needed a bigger number. The next time we raised money was the IPO. Ultimately, we didn't actually raise very much money. I think the total equity was $41 million or $44 million.

Regarding the IPO, once people saw that the company was stable, the very second they saw it was stable, there were discussions about an IPO. At the time, there wasn't a lot of success in healthcare IT – probably none. athena was really the first IPO in read/write Internet healthcare. It was probably the second IPO and read/write business at all. (There was Ariba, which is another great one to study because they were the first read/write Internet company to go public. They weren't just looking something up but actually doing workflow over this clunky, slow Internet.) And so, I said, "Look, I'm not doing it until I have a portfolio of products, so I can have ways of getting to the number, a portfolio of markets and profitability." And I got two of the three. I wasn't profitable in public, but I knew it was in the bag for the first quarter after. I think we went public with $100 million in revenue and no profit. But in the next quarter, we had profit, and we never didn't after that. As for our mission, I feel like missions are like surfing. It's not a mode of transportation. You get up on the board, and the way it ends is you crash into the beach, and you get up. You go back out, and you try to go a little longer. That's it, right?

These corporate missions are the same way. It's more like rules for travel – how to travel – more than how we're going to get there. I could see accomplishments along the way, toward the goal and toward the grand vision. We wanted to be the healthcare Internet, and we were not; they're not. It's not. Medical records are all separate stacks, and they make billions and billions of dollars of profit. And that brings happiness to all the struggling waifs at Bain Capital and Hellman & Friedman and all these needy mouths that they feed.

But the thought was that these 100,000 doctors could see the same logical object and build rather than duplicate. And it is still not the case for doctors today on the Internet. They are duplicating – duplicating like mad all day long, maybe 20% less than they would be if they weren't on athenaNet. I don't know what their latest measures are and how they count the clicks and all that.

Either way, it was progress against that. It was a gateway drug or fertilizer – use your favorite metaphor. We tacked in the right direction, with lots of leaked wind and lots of missed days and missed turning points. But I feel that it was good, and I think, probably most satisfyingly from a mission perspective, was that we impregnated 5,000 people with a belief in doing things that had no precedent in healthcare. The idea of health tech as a category at all was groundbreaking. As a category, certainly that would attract people out of Stanford – the best and brightest types saying, "I don't want to work at McKinsey. I want to go work at athenahealth." What?

We had a "fondest wish" exercise: in 20 years, when you look back what will it be?

That came from our first retreat. We had a "fondest wish" exercise: in 20 years, when you look back, what will it be? One person said, "We are going to be on the cover of the Wall Street Journal, as the savior of some data outage or something." Another said, "We're going to have a Super Bowl ad." Another was, "We're going to be a better job on your resume then McKinsey in healthcare." And this last one was from a group of founders who had all gone to Booz Allen, which was sort of the "less-than" McKinsey consulting. The fact that you could do high-level work, make high-level pay, and have it immediately be of consequence, as opposed to turning in a PowerPoint-bound volume that would sit in a lateral sliding file drawer at a bank or whatever, really mattered.

If you look at the list of executives from *Forbes* or *Fortune* or all these digital health companies, I mean, they're all being led by Athenistas [what athenahealth employees call themselves]. And if not the top job, other key jobs. So, I feel like that was accomplished, but again, that's like surfing. We had a lot of good runs at the beach.

In truth, focus on jobs that people hate and suck at.

To other founders, I say, do a job following the Jobs to Be Done[12] approach. In truth, focus on jobs that people hate and suck at. It has to be both because if they suck at it, but they think they're kind of cool at it, they will keep doing it. Take the poor guy who wants to mow my lawn. I suck at mowing my lawn. But I love mowing my lawn. I imagine someday I'll get my own tractor, but now I'm pushing the electric thing. The guy is asking me, "You sure you don't want me to mow?" And I'm thinking, I know he should do it because he's better at it, but I really like mowing my lawn.

Doctors also run into that a lot. They don't want you taking over their clinical decision support with maternity care.

If you do a job, choose one that people hate and suck at, and do it with your heart, putting love into it.

One final thought: if you do a job, choose one that people hate and suck at, *and* do it with your heart, putting love into it. There's an alchemy where this shitty work has this magic glow to it. I can still go to this mail processing center that exists. I live in Maine, and two hours from here is the operation center, where a tractor-trailer, still today, has mail arrive every morning in the dark to this freaking building. In the back are all these carts of mail, and these people (70% women and 30% men) open a tractor-trailer full of mail. They figure out what it is. Take the staples out, scan it, and store it so that they can find it again. And the energy in that room is unbelievable! Because they love it!

Charles Royce eventually had his own manor house, even though he was a mechanic. He had etched onto his big, walk-in fireplace:

He who does his work with honor, no matter how humble, is noble.

He was not a noble but was living in a nobleman's home.

I think that that's the last piece of advice: if you put your heart into it, that will feel good to a lot of people, and you will get much more than their market wage out of them. And you won't feel bad about it.

3.5 Notes

____

____

____

____

____

____

Endnotes

1 https://www.athenahealth.com/
2 athenahealth – Wikipedia.
3 https://my.pitchbook.com/profile/12858-31/company/deals
4 https://en.wikipedia.org/wiki/IDX_Systems
5 https://www.cbsnews.com/news/mckesson-in-14b-health-merger/
6 A *tablespace* is a storage location where the actual data underlying database objects can be kept. It provides a layer of abstraction between physical and logical data[1] and serves to allocate storage for all DBMS-managed segments. (A database segment is a database object that occupies physical space, such as table data and indexes.) Once created, a tablespace can be referred to by name when creating database segments. https://en.wikipedia.org/wiki/Tablespace
7 Whys is the practice of asking *why* repeatedly whenever a problem is encountered to get beyond the obvious symptoms to discover the root cause. https://www.lean.org/lexicon-terms/5-whys/
8 More details on the HITECH Act here https://www.hipaajournal.com/what-is-the-hitech-act/
9 More details on Michael Porter's strategy specifically about location, here https://hbr.org/1998/11/clusters-and-the-new-economics-of-competition
10 More on Edward Schein's approach to organizational culture https://mitsloan.mit.edu/ideas-made-to-matter/5-enduring-management-ideas-mit-sloans-edgar-schein
11 More on Soc2 here https://www.aicpa-cima.com/topic/audit-assurance/audit-and-assurance-greater-than-soc-2
12 More on Jobs to Be Done https://hbr.org/2016/09/know-your-customers-jobs-to-be-done

Chapter 4

ConcertAI

It's like you're constantly looking forward, left and right, and slightly behind you. (You hope behind you, as you are building.) Ideally, you want to get something in the hands of people you are trying to serve, whether it's early code, or your production solution.

– Jeff Elton, Founder and CEO

4.1 Quick Facts

Website	https://www.concertai.com/
Founded	2017
Mission	*Our mission is to accelerate insights and improve outcomes for patients through leading real-world data, AI technologies, and scientific expertise in partnership with the leading biomedical innovators, healthcare providers, and medical societies.*[1]
Founders	Jeff Elton https://www.linkedin.com/in/jelton/ Romesh Wadhwani https://www.linkedin.com/in/romesh-wadhwani/
Unicorn status achieved	2022

 DOI: 10.4324/9781032711034-4

Funding rounds[2]	Three funding deals • December 2017–March 2022 • PE and VC; VC $300M
Notable funders	• SAIGroup (Acquirer of two entities, former ASCO CancerLinQ agreement, and provided "A Series" financing) • Declaration Partners (Led "B" Series) • Maverick Ventures • AllianceBernstein • Sixth Street Partners (Sole investor of Series C)

4.2 TDLR

Ideate

- Founded by Jeff Elton and Romesh Wadhwani, head of Symphony AI (now SAIGroup)
- Focus on AI, machine learning, and large-scale multi-modal data with applications in healthcare and life sciences
- Oncology chosen due to having the greatest depth and breadth of real-world data from national cancer initiatives and because oncology is approximately 40% of all R&D investment, has the highest number of new drug approvals of any disease, and is 90% of accelerated approval therapeutics
- Operates at the intersection of two ecosystems: healthcare providers and life sciences
- Use of deep, multimodal data and AI for insights

Build

- Multi-year agreement with the American Society of Clinical Oncology (ASCO) in late 2017
- Focus on unstructured data from electronic medical records; acquired CancerLinQ from ASCO in December of 2023; partnership agreements with more than 100 other clinical providers and research sites
- Use of small language models, large language models, agentic AI, and natural language processing models (processed through the CARAai™ Generative and Agentic AI platform) and human data curation

- Board partnership to "complete the patient journey" with Caris Life Sciences, NeoGenomics, Guardant, PathAI, and others put into place in late 2022 through early 2025
- Broad collaboration with NVIDIA around the CARAai applications in clinical trials and other areas formed in 2024
- Strategy to share with prospective partners
- Secured agreements with companies like Bristol Myers Squibb, AbbVie, and J&J

Launch

- Delivered first functionalities in mid-2019
- Focused on non-small cell lung cancer, small cell lung cancer, breast cancer, colorectal cancer, and multiple myeloma
- Launched Discovery platform for AI insights
- Expanded customer base and completed Series B funding round
- Maintained growth through the pandemic with cloud-based infrastructure

Grow

- Expanded customer base and product offerings
- Launched clinical trial solutions
- Continued innovation and data as-a-service subscriptions
- Completed Series C funding round in 2022, raising $150 million
- Achieved a $1.9 billion valuation
- Focus on regulatory fitness and evolving solutions

4.3 Meet the Founder

Jeff Elton, PhD, is vice chairman and founding CEO of ConcertAI, a generative and agentic AI Software-as-a-Service (SaaS) solutions company providing oncology research and patient-centric solutions for life sciences innovators and the world's leading healthcare providers. The company has leading-in-class AI solutions for multi-modal clinical oncology research from translational phase through post-approval; AI SaaS for oncology clinical trials; patient-centric SaaS for specialty pharmacy therapeutics; oncology clinical pathways; and radiological interpretation and clinical AI. Solutions are deployed within the top 50 biopharma and more than 2,000 healthcare providers globally.

Founded in 2018, the company has grown every year and became EBITDA positive in Q4 of 2024. In December of 2023, ConcertAI acquired CancerLinQ, previously part of the American Society of Clinical Oncology (ASCO), as the largest multi-EMR clinical network in the United States. Major strategic partnerships are in place with NVIDIA, Caris Life Sciences, Guardant, NeoGenomics, and PathAI. The company is headquartered in Cambridge, MA, and has just over 1,000 employees, with more than 30% having advanced clinical or scientific degrees.

Jeff Elton

Prior to ConcertAI, Jeff was managing director at Accenture Strategy/Patient Health, global chief operating officer and SVP of strategy at Novartis Institutes of BioMedical Research, Inc., and partner at McKinsey & Company. Jeff is currently vice chairman of the Board of the Massachusetts Biotechnology Council. He is the co-author of the widely cited book, *Healthcare Disrupted* (Wiley, 2016), and has been quoted or the focus of more than 100 articles and podcasts over the last several years. Jeff has a PhD and MBA from the University of Chicago.

4.4 Interview with Jeff Elton, Founding CEO

ConcertAI was built by our chairman, Romesh Wadhwani, and me. Romesh is the founder of the private equity group SymphonyAI (now SAI Group) and a past co-founder of Symphony Technology Group. For SAI Group, ConcertAI was a new form of venture. Historically, Romesh was a private equity investor, focused on the acquisition and value enhancement of existing companies. But with SAI Group, Romesh was focused on the enormous value and business model transformation he believed would come from AI and machine learning Software-as-a-Service (SaaS) solutions. With the emerging generation of AI, there was an opportunity to rethink how different parts of different industries and businesses were run. So, as we sat down and talked about it, healthcare was an obvious place to start, given the enormous amount of data that is captured on a patient's clinical journey and all financial aspects of healthcare. So, from the very beginning, both healthcare and life sciences became a deep focus.

> ***[T]his concept of being a trusted intermediary between two ecosystems, healthcare providers on one hand and life sciences on the other, was a concept that was part of the company from the very beginning.***

Interestingly, this concept of being a trusted intermediary between two ecosystems, healthcare providers on one hand and life sciences on the other, was a concept that was part of the company from the very beginning. Furthermore, oncology emerged also because of the level and depth of data and information from cancer care, which is much greater as a result of the National Cancer Institute initiatives. And there are other national initiatives, US government initiatives, indicating that there is molecular genomic data that addresses the underlying biological basis of a tumor. About 40% of the clinical development in the pipeline at the industry level is focused on oncology, in part because there's more information about disease biology. So, people have more confidence in doing their R&D in this area. From the very beginning, there were a few themes that we knew were going to be part of our work. One part was that it was going to involve deep, rich, multimodal data and gleaning actionable insights from these data. Another was that it was going to involve an ecosystem of healthcare providers and an ecosystem of biopharma innovators, working with AI SaaS solutions, that together would enable the acceleration of needed new medicines for patients' highest unmet medical needs.

> ***[W]e knew from the beginning that AI would be critical.***

AI and machine learning, inherent in our name, were a part of how we thought we could take super-complicated data at a population scale. For cancer patients, there may be billions of data points for individual patients over the course of their treatment and long-term surveillance of their outcomes. Much of this is "unstructured" in that it is not machine readable. This would include notes, PDFs, documents, and other sources. As it turns out, most of the concepts you need to diagnose, create a treatment plan, and assess the effectiveness of a treatment are in these data. Therefore, we knew from the beginning that AI would be critical. To do this manually would require thousands of human curators and years of time. Our early goal was to provide highly trusted and high-veracity data at scale as a service to enable healthcare and life researchers to generate insights more rapidly, assess their consistency with peer-reviewed literature, and then initiate studies and analyses that would end up as publications further extending and enhancing the evidence we have. In many cases, the users of our solutions are making observations that are not currently in the literature. Clinical and scientific literature presents a confirmation of what we know, whereas most of what will ultimately be known is not currently known. AI presents the opportunity to infer relationships and identify characteristics outside of current published materials while also contextualizing other insights relative to highly respected and peer-reviewed sources. What is even more powerful is the establishment of causality versus correlations – that is, the power of new AI approaches. This, in turn, allows us to advance validations of these new insights and translate them into recommendations, actions, or implications.

Early in ConcertAI's history, we put together a multi-year agreement with ASCO's[3] CancerLinQ program to provide expertise, technologies, and services to challenges of processing healthcare data. There are generally two forms of health data that are frequently accessed: medical claims and electronic medical records. If you want to know what the outcomes are for people with low-acuity chronic diseases (e.g., diabetes and cardiovascular disease), you can glean that from medical claims data because you'll see their consumption resources, additional therapeutics added to their treatment, or transitions in treatment. For example, for individuals with diabetes, which is a very long progressive disease, you'll see the different phases of somebody going from metformin to injected insulin or GLP-1s.

Oncology is very different. Some cancers progress rapidly, are generally quite acute, and involve a significant level of clinical intensity. The most critical oncology data sits in what's called unstructured data. It's in medical oncologist, radiologist, and pathologist notes and reports appended to the medical record. For example, if the patient received a next-generation sequencing molecular diagnostic report, it goes into the EMR as a PDF. If you get a radiologist's interpretation report, it goes into the EMR as a PDF. (The fact that radiological interpretations begin as speech-to-text data that would be machine readable but end up as unstructured data is a source of some frustration!)

When you begin pulling this all together, about 70% of the concepts of interest come out of these unstructured data sources, which is a challenge for the provider delivering care and everybody else engaged in clinical research. So, when we approached this, we knew that deriving insights out of this unstructured data was going to be a critical part of this process.

> ***Regulatory and other oncology research required covering hundreds of concepts and very complex concepts.***

At the time when we started the company, the term "natural language processing" existed, but the accuracy and recall of the models were below research standards, the cost of running those models was high, and the process was slow. And the number of concepts that you would be able to derive out of them was relatively narrow, largely comprised of lab values across different diagnostic reports – in the end only 20 to 30 concepts or variable categories. Regulatory and other oncology research required covering hundreds of concepts and very complex concepts.

Higher performance and reliable data sets were created through human curation – a process where business rules were based on generally accepted standards for deriving critical concepts from unstructured data. The only way to create data sets machines could read and analyses could be performed. The AI of the period of 2019 provided high utility in very niche areas. For example, non-small cell lung cancer is 85% of lung cancers, but it doesn't have an ICD code. Therefore, a machine or an analyst can determine the status of a patient in the traditional fashion. As a reminder, none of that information sits in medical claims data. Medical claims data can't tell you anything about the outcomes, can't tell you anything about the stage of the patient, and can't tell you anything about the line of therapy. However, we could create an AI model accessible to the researcher capable of making this determination on the fly. So, this is still in use today.

So, you have these incredible gaps in everything that you see and do, which actually make it very difficult for a biopharma innovator to design a study, assess the effectiveness of a drug that is approved, or do ongoing surveillance of safety. For healthcare providers, it's no wonder they have to go through all this data with clinical supporting personnel, sometimes reading through 20 to 30 tabs in an individual patient's record. It's extremely time-consuming, as well as something that doesn't allow them to integrate all the data sources as they would like to, as efficiently as they need to.

While we knew all this when we set up the company, for example, having periods of manual processing that was not the vision of what we were working toward. The concept for the company was to create a set of products that would become an essential part of the workflows of life science companies and healthcare providers, as both AI software-as-a-service [SaaS] and data-as-a-service are provided on a subscription basis, assuring high recurring revenues and high forward visibility. We had a road map that always extended three years ahead. Aside from contributing to the stability of the company, this allowed us to make focused investments, ahead of others, that ensured higher value to our customers and higher benefit to patients.

> ***We knew we had to start with data – any AI company that is building a domain specific solution needs to have access to the highest quantity, depth, and representative data available.***

We knew we had to start with data – any AI company that is building a domain specific solution needs to have access to the highest quantity, depth, and representative data available. We also knew we had to have credibility in the underlying concepts of what we were building such that the results of analyses or recommendations could be accepted without secondary review that took as long as primary analysis! The big change was that we were not focused on projects. Everything going on in the field at the time were expensive projects that provided meaningful insights but really didn't build a capability or capacity that you could scale. Consequently, nothing changed in how the work itself was done.

> ***The reason why we were interested in AI is it could change the work and business processes, and most importantly change the outcomes realized from the work.***

The reason why we were interested in AI is that it could change the work and business processes, and most importantly, change the outcomes realized from the work. And that was the contribution we wanted to make, whether it was for clinical development or standard of care or clinical decision augmentation tools.

About six months into 2018, my chairman and I wrote the strategy for the company, articulating what it was going to be in a form that could be shared with prospective partners. We had a very different way of thinking about things, which was that we were going to articulate where we were going and look for our first partners to be those who said, "You got it right and we're really excited about that."

> ***The first agreements we wrote were "forward buys" of what the road map said we would deliver.***

The first agreements we wrote were "forward buys" of what the road map said we would deliver. But we had credibility based on what our people had accomplished in the past – building businesses, delivering solutions, and doing significant things before ConcertAI. Some of the parties we were interacting with knew that I had delivered and done things before at scale, and Romesh had as well. So, there was confidence, but there wasn't any payment for the things we hadn't delivered; rather, an obligation to pay for it once we delivered it and met reasonable acceptance criteria. We had multiple early lighthouse partners who entered into these three-year forward agreements. In fact, if you look back at our press releases, you'll see companies like Bristol Myers Squibb, AbbVie, J&J, and others. So, we had multiple companies that said, "Yeah, you got it right. That's a great strategy, if you can actually deliver as you say you're going to."

Not that this was an easy process, as all of them required us to use our P&L. They didn't fund the concept or new product development, and we weren't asking them to fund it. We basically said, "We'll take the obligation to invest and build. You're taking the obligation to receive it once it's built."

The A funding round was all made by SymphonyAI, plus we had some base revenues from some of the early work we were doing. But now, we really forced ourselves to focus on those offerings that we were going to be of value for our partners.

> ***We were constantly evaluating where we were versus the market, because things change in the course of 2 or 3 years.***

It's important to note that we didn't and still don't exist in a vacuum. Other people are trying to do some innovative things in the world of oncology. We position ourselves as an oncology research and standard-of-care solutions company. We were constantly evaluating where we were versus the market because things change in the course of two or three years. It's like you're constantly looking forward, left and right, and slightly behind you. (You *hope* behind you as you are building.) Ideally, you want to get something in the hands of people you are trying to serve, whether it's early code or your production solution. Rapidly prototyping and putting something in the hands of the ultimate customers, which establishes a view of the actual functionalities of what you are building, is critical. You can describe something in words and PowerPoint, but now that you've got something that's palpable in front of people, their sense of what they need actually changes versus what they were able to articulate before. So, it's not just market changes but also people using the tools that they didn't have previously, changing what they want from the tool. So, you've got these kinds of forces going in a couple of different directions.

We are now getting toward the latter part of 2018, and the first agreements were in place in January through March of 2019. The first delivery of the initial functionalities, akin to what we've contracted, started in August and September of 2019. This included our new data-as-a-service, data sets, and insights into a few specific disease areas. Breast cancer was the first one we tackled, followed by non-small cell lung cancer. We had our first technology platform, which was called Eureka Discovery at the time, which was designed to glean insights. It had a reasonable amount of AI in production, which few other companies had at the time.

By the time we got to the end of 2019, we were pretty fortunate. We expanded our customer base, and we saw the first revenues from our new solutions. We did our Series B funding at the end of 2019, so we were moving pretty rapidly. While revenues were growing at a higher double-digit rate, we were EBITDA-negative, as you would imagine. The B series included Declaration Partners as the lead investor, with Maverick Ventures and Alliance Bernstein all becoming investors. That was an $85–86 million raise with a post-evaluation of over $850 million. When you think about where we are now, economic periods were a little bit different, valuations were a bit different, but we were in an area that had a lot of interest and had established early leadership. We were demonstrating the ability to execute on forward, recurring contracts, which not very many people were doing. We weren't very far into those contracts, but they did have three-year durations, and we were in the first few months of delivery against them.

So, we had commercial credibility and multiple pharmaceutical manufacturers working with us. We also had a *very* large amount of data accessible to us as a result of doing work with the ASCO CancerLinQ[4] program at the time, which was also a fairly unique position. We were performing services for them as part of our investment in the agreement with them, in addition to some cash payments to ASCO itself. But we were also able to derive a level of insight, data, and access to data that was representative of many aspects of oncology care in this country.

> ***From the outset, we have always worked under Business Associate Agreements[5] [BAAs].***

From the outset, we have always worked under Business Associate Agreements[6] [BAAs]. And under those agreements, there are conditions for interacting with fully identifiable data that are specified by the US Health and Human Services Department and stipulate the work you can do in research and quality of care. So, there are boundary conditions about what we're doing, and we obviously respect those. All our work was for ASCO in some of their quality programs, which at the time were called QOPI.[7]

> ***Once we knew what the use cases were, we'd create the deidentified data set aligned to that use.***

We did a lot of work supporting those programs. Any other data we used had very clear parameters and had to be research-focused. (Research in this context, just to be clear, has a very specific meaning: you're taking a cohort or a population, you specify the questions you're going to ask, and the likely uses for the research are going into a medical society meeting, an abstract, or a poster session. Ideally, you're trying to get it into a peer-reviewed journal and say, "Yes, I made a contribution to the field.") We only built solutions with fully HIPAA-compliant deidentified data. Once we knew what the use cases were, we'd create the deidentified dataset aligned to that use.

Now at this point in our history, we weren't linking molecular data. We were pulling all the data from different sources within the electronic medical record environment. But think about other companies that had started prior to us – they were not AI-centric. Roche has a division called Flatiron with one central EMR, so they derived data from their own EMR, OncoEMR.[8] A division of McKesson was doing something similar. All our competitors were owned by very large companies. McKesson's EMR was iKnowMed [now part of McKesson's Ontada division[9]]. The data that we were bringing together represented about ten EMRs, which included Epic, Cerner, MOSAIQ, ARIA from Varian, and a lot of specialty ones for oncology.

We also included data from academic centers, although most of the data that was available at the time was community-based. Typically, you would go to a single academic center and collaborate with them on getting a single data set. In contrast, the data that we were beginning to gather included multiple academic centers, regional health systems, and community providers. So, we could get data for all different care settings, and we were able to build a disease registry model and monitor standard-of-care changes, new diagnostic modalities, and new drug approvals. We also made sure that whatever we were representing with that data represented the contemporary standard of care in all care settings and across all 50 states.

And that's something we tried to do from the very beginning, which goes back to my initial comments about trying to make this reference-grade from the beginning. We didn't want to focus just on "Can we do it?" but instead on, "Can we do something that materially changes insights with a high confidence level and veracity that a clinician would act upon it?" The advantage of doing this health research in the United States is that HIPAA is specific and very uniform. If you go to other regions of the world, say if you're looking at Europe and European privacy rules, European privacy rules have a very high bar. It's a bit counter to the way that a lot of things are in Europe, but European privacy rules put a very large responsibility on the data controller. Oftentimes each controller, which could be an individual hospital, develops their own version of how they're doing it. And they're always stricter – very detailed, very narrow. So, everything there tends to be federated [architectures] because you can't move anything anywhere. The problem with a federated architecture,[10] when you have different rules of engagement at every single point of the federation, is the abstraction is either up so high (Is it really worth it? Am I getting anything of value?) or the abstraction layer is down low, requiring an individual sign-off by every single institution. And that gets complicated. I know, because I've done it. I ran a program, before starting this company, where we did the same program in the United States and Europe, but with very different approaches.

For ConcertAI, everything was built as centralized here [US] in a HIPAA- and HITRUST-certified cloud environment.

For ConcertAI, everything was built as centralized here [US] in a HIPAA- and HITRUST-certified cloud environment. At the time, the state of the art was to build an environment that allowed us to bring in identifiable data. But usually, the way these architectures are set up is the data is encrypted in transit and encrypted at rest; data can enter, but you limit access and egress. So basically, we had very strict rules to create abstracted and de-identified data. To pull the feature out, there would be a separate environment that would also be highly controlled, and that highly controlled data would only allow in records that were going to be acted upon immediately. You act, you abstract, you use your natural language processing, you deidentify the data, and you can then move deidentified data out of that environment. What you've effectively done is create an area where things can go in, but nothing can come out, except one pipe to a processing area with no retention.

As we start moving into a generative AI world, I think the world is reevaluating this how to bring data back together. Generative AI requires a very different way of thinking about data. Don't think about data as departments as they are represented today with different enterprise solutions. Because generative AI can establish a context around the flow of what it's seeing, and you can, through different orchestrations, like agent orchestrations, process data even from multiple modalities, which tend to come from multiple "departments" or even enterprise solutions. That's a real challenge for a lot of companies. The logical architecture of these domains and data is very specific to the group and the function, and oftentimes even the application layer sitting on top of that.

We had the advantage early on of having an AI-friendly environment. In fact, you'll find if you scan [on the Internet] a joint publication[11] that was done with ASCO CancerLinQ, a couple other parties, and ConcertAI, documenting that in an environment like that you can bring state-of-the-art natural language processing and AI capabilities to make unstructured data available almost on demand. It was probably one of the biggest and greatest illustrations of using data from multiple data sources in different ways, and we are now taking a look at population scale for doing the same thing. We got that into a published manuscript and a few other things.

> ***There's this tension about protecting intellectual property and keeping everything silent and opaque.***

There's this tension about protecting intellectual property and keeping everything silent and opaque. Because if you do that, oftentimes it's viewed as a black box, and people don't like using outcomes from black boxes. Technology is going to move very rapidly; therefore, what you say and what you publish already has its own timeline. By the time the research makes its way through the peer review process and appears, you're already on to the next generation anyway.

We decided early on in our history to be transparent. We publish a lot about how and what we do. As an example, at the last ASCO meeting, we presented our clinical trial patient matching and prioritization models and overarching approach. We are saying, "Dispel the mystery to increase the confidence using our solution because we are going to be moving on to the next thing anyway." Catch us if you can, kind of thing.

So, now we're in B series and going into 2020, and we're still slightly pre-pandemic. We continue to advance our data-as-a-service subscriptions, expand our team, and I think we had about 14 customers at the time. We're feeling super good, and you know, we had three or four customers – not just one – that were large – and 15 smaller ones. And when you are fundraising, the prospective funders always ask, "Did you find one person that really likes what you are doing, and is that what's funding everything?" If the answer is "yes," whoever the individual executive is could leave, making everyone feel very vulnerable. We worked pretty hard to make sure there was diversity in the customer base. In contrast today, by the way, we have 47 life sciences companies that use our solutions in some fashion. Most of them have been through their second, if not third, renewals. In terms of providers, we have some outstanding numbers there too. We have about 1,900 healthcare providers who use our technologies, and those 1,900 are paying – this isn't a freemium model. They see the value that we deliver.

From 2019 to 2021, we continued to expand our customer base and our product offerings. We were just starting to launch the first version of our clinical trials solution to do study design, and we had a road map for clinical development. Then the pandemic started. But for us, we were born a cloud company, a digital company, and our infrastructure was common from the beginning. In fact, all our infrastructure was cloud. Even our business processes were all cloud. For us, it really didn't impact the cultural side of the business and didn't really impact the other parts of the business either.

> ***In certain areas, like in our radiological imaging, we have low, single-digit contract churn rate. It's a pretty outstanding level of customer retention.***

We continued to grow every year. It depends on the year, but in the earlier years we were growing 40% to 60% per year, and as we get up to a larger size, we've always been somewhere in the 25%+ range of growth year over year. We've not had a down year (knock on wood) in our history, which we appreciate. Our customers have confidence in us to stay with us. In certain areas, like in our radiological imaging, we have a low, single-digit contract churn rate. It's a pretty outstanding level of customer retention.

While you never do exactly as much as you'd like to do, I think part of the reason we are able to have a low churn rate is because we spend a lot of time understanding the strategies of our customers and where they are going and do our best to support those strategies. Just to give you an idea, when we go to the JP Morgan Healthcare Conference, the American Society of Hematology meetings, ASCO meetings, etc., we are alarmingly transparent with our customers about what we're planning and where we are. And we lay it out in detail. Even today, we're a private company, but when we meet with customers, oftentimes on the first page, I'm giving them a financial summary of the company. Even when the pandemic came, I gave people advanced notice of what the operating model was going to be and why we chose that operating model. We have a lot of epidemiologists. And this is a disease. So, I asked our epidemiologists, "How is this going to play out?" And they said, "Not well, and it's going to take a long time." And I'm like, "OK, well, I don't really need any more analysis than that." I'm going to assume it's going to take us a year or two, so let me put my one-year or two-year strategy into place. We wrote to all our customers within 48 hours and told them what we were going to do, effective this date. Weirdly, we were probably one of the first virtual companies going to customers and sharing our plan. What was interesting was all our customers shared their plans and what they were thinking about doing to cope with the pandemic, too.

The reason why I even tell the story down to that level is to show how we operate and how it affects future investment by customers. I've literally had customers say,

> *Jeff, maybe you have some customers who really value these things that you're telling me about. But these two reasons that you just articulated – these are enormously important to us. These will change the decisions we make internally, how we prioritize, and how we operate.*

So, from our vantage point, that's great, and we're right there aligned with our customers. We have always been focused not only on delivering against our strategy but also on staying forward-thinking and responsive to our customers.

If you were looking at my computer desktop right now (which is a good thing you're not, because it's a mess, perhaps a reflection of my life, really), there's a note that we're drafting internally. We are re-platforming aspects of our cloud, where our AI lives. We've got a new strategy that we call CARAai™,[12] which has a very different view on the data layer, different latency and refresh rate of data, more continuous processing of unstructured data, and a series of large language models and other services. On top are multi-generative AI, agentic AI, and assistants, just to pick a name that's really familiar to you. But change is hard, even for a more entrepreneurial organization, because of the pace of technological change we are seeing in the marketplace. We had a bunch of ConcertAI team members asking, "If I'm not working on generative AI, does it mean I'm working on something that's just going to disappear?"

It probably should have been obvious to me that this would become a concern. So, the note we are drafting is to answer that question with a "no." Solutions that people use in their everyday work go through evolutions, and those evolutions have different speeds at which they evolve. And your job right now is to support the evolutions. We're going to see, even within the context of our current solutions, aspects of that data layer adding more, but generative AI may start as an interface layer, and then eventually, the orchestration layer will change. This is going to evolve very rapidly, and we're actually going to go, for certain solutions, to a quarterly release cycle. A couple of other solutions will have a twice-a-year cycle because they're operating in a regulated environment. But some of our solutions are now going to go to a 30–60-day release cycle because the pace of technology will allow that.

> ***This idea of evolutionary product planning was not something anybody really thought about, even a little bit. It's one of those concepts that we developed with our customers, and we bring them into the process as well.***

This idea of evolutionary product planning was not something anybody really thought about, even a little bit. It's one of those concepts that we developed with our customers, and we bring them into the process as well. We continued to grow through the pandemic, and our last and third financing round, which was a Series C round, was in 2022. We closed it in February or March of 2022. We had thought we were going to do the round and close it at the end of 2021. That would have been almost exactly two years after our Series B. And if you recall anything about the markets at the time, it was a very uncertain period. But it hadn't become clear that it was going to become this period, which would wipe out some valuations to the degree that it did. We were doing very well and entered a couple of new areas, enabling us to continue to grow.

As we're working with multiple alternative investors considering our C round, their respective investment committees were meeting *daily*; they were watching and wanted to know what we would be doing. Historically, these are weekly meetings, but they were meeting daily. You have these experiences, and you're looking at it, reviewing the runway ahead of you, the market dynamics, and running different scenarios in your mind. Then you close the round, the money appears in your bank accounts, and you say to yourself, "OK, I learned a lot. That was a little hairier than we wanted it to be, but it's done." We knew we wanted to get it done in 2021 and not wait until 2022. But everybody was watching the market dynamics very closely. You're not the one controlling the timeline, and your prospective investors are trying to make sure it's something they really want to do. The investors were 6th St. Partners, and the round was a $150 million Series C, and that was when we ended up with a $1.9 billion valuation. As you know, we've subsequently integrated two other organizations into ConcertAI and TeraRecon, which focuses on radiological imaging visualization and AI interpretations, and then the CancerLinQ entity for real-world data.

> ***We've always had this view that we don't take any of these successes for granted. Whether it's an investor or a new contract for us, it represents another commitment we've made to drive value in those organizations.***

But fortunately, we did honor the plan and the things we said we would do. The investors have done well, and we've done well, too. We've always had this view that we don't take any of these successes for granted. Whether it's an investor or a new contract for us, it represents another commitment we've made to drive value in those organizations. We're very aware of our commitments, and we're very aware of what we said we would do and try to deliver.

> ***We would rather rip up our own playbook than have outside forces do it for us.***

Which brings us to one of the reasons why we're departing from our own playbook right now: we would rather rip up our own playbook than have outside forces do it for us. We've done a year and a quarter of AI experiments. We've taken every single aspect of our operation and tested multiple alternative AI LLM and LRM technologies, creating bootstrap versions of different parts of our company off in this secure zone. We've done all these experiments and came away saying, "All right, this is truly different. This is not hype." Cost performance is truly different; functionality, capabilities, and speed of inference and response are exceptional and different. Enough so, in a super cool way, I think it actually is an accelerator to get to the things we thought we wanted to do when we start putting the company together. But also, it's hard for people to rip up a playbook and rethink things. Again, we're six years old; we haven't been here that long. I can only imagine if I were running a multibillion-dollar organization that had been around for 40 years, I'd probably be a little shell-shocked, trying to do some of this stuff.

When we reached Unicorn status, we felt we now had some control over our destiny. By now, we have a board and a responsibility to them and customer agreements. But when we did the raise, it was designed to get us to the point where we would be EBITDA-positive and cash flow positive. So, it's an arc of a trajectory that would feel good to move through.

To this day, we are people that, when the money comes in, we view it as a commitment, because we put a business case in front of our investors.

At that point – and again, we were literally monitoring bank accounts to make sure that the money was there – we had this moment of pause – reflection and acceptance – and *appreciation* that we could take everything to the next level, to where we want to go. That's wonderful and humbling and warm. You don't get to stay in that moment very long, but it is a moment when, if you don't feel it, you're really missing something. It's truly reinforcing what you're going to be doing next. To this day, we are people who, when the money comes in, we view it as a commitment, because we put a business case in front of our investors.

Sometimes, I've worked with direct competitors to get something done that otherwise couldn't get done. Solemn commitments force you to put a few parts of yourself aside to move some things forward.

Things do change, but that doesn't mean your commitments change. You actually have to figure out different ways to honor those commitments, regardless. If I have a contract commitment to a customer, I may have a hiccup or conundrum or thought I was going to have a flow of data or capabilities that I don't; that's not their problem. If I have a hiccup, that's my problem. We've always taken our obligations in that respect – they are solemn commitments. I think because we did that, it forced us to resolve the problems in different ways. Sometimes, I've worked with direct competitors to get something done that otherwise couldn't get done. Solemn commitments force you to put a few parts of yourself aside to move some things forward.

Bottom line: achieving Unicorn status was recognized and appreciated, and I would say the moment is even appreciated now. Without that achievement, we probably wouldn't be where we are. In the second half of this year, each of our product areas should be EBITDA-positive on a stand-alone basis. The year overall should be slightly EBITDA-positive on a consolidated basis, and we will be nominally cash positive. And our contracts are multi-year, so that means we have visibility to late 2025, 2026, and to the beginning of 2027. We're taking a pretty hard look at that to understand where we want that to go.

The solutions we have are very specialized, focused on oncology, which is deeply scientific and has clinical attributes that are used by healthcare providers as well as the clinical development, translational medicine, medical, and epidemiology functions in pharmaceutical companies. When we look at what we are now comparatively, we started off with highly focused and more niche solutions that experts would use. If you look at our road map (and some of this, we haven't kind of released fully publicly but have started to socialize it), I have ten articulated assistants off our CARAai platform coming out for different domains. One of them, we are using ourselves, internally, to run part of our business. Then it will be migrated into being an offering for our customers.

As we begin doing that, many of these move up to a different vantage point in the enterprise, and they're actually used by different user personas, but they interrelate to each other. While this has its own risk and pivot, there is excitement and value, too. But there's a view that if you get to rethink the work and you get to rethink how decisions can be made and where they're made, that's part of the value that comes from the deep, rich, first-party data and some of the technologies being deployed. That's what's exciting!

But that's also part of growing up. You learn a lot about the domain you're operating in, and you learn there are ways to

add more value, but you're also moving up to the level of some other players that you haven't been interacting with before.

We're evolving, as I mentioned before; it's an evolutionary path. Some of these evolutions are things we've never done before, coming into workflows where historically we may not have been, but all of them interrelate to each other. But that's also part of growing up. You learn a lot about the domain you're operating in, and you learn there are ways to add more value, but you're also moving up to the level of some other players that you haven't been interacting with before.

[J]ust because we know we can do it, and just because we think it makes sense, doesn't make it a product.

You can't under-collect market feedback, input, and reactions to what you're trying. We have an internal incubation process. All ideas go through a vetting process, and every new thing we do goes through this process. It starts with all sorts of interviews, interactions, feedback, and responses; just because we know we can do it, and just because we think it makes sense, doesn't make it a product. We have to work our way through that. In fact, the call I was on before talking to you was literally looking at the first results out of an incubation process. And I'd say it was going OK, but we learned some things. I think even if the incubation process pivots, the process requires discipline, which is needed. You get the concept, the economics, and the market timing, and the market timing matters *tremendously*.

So, you get these different vantage points on what you're doing. And it's super important that if you don't have the legitimate right and the perceived credibility and everything else to bring this forward, it's probably not you who should be using your scarce capital resources and talent.

The second area is, once you go through that process, build something as quickly as possible – get under the hood of the problem. Even if you're in a consulting services business, it's going to be supported by technology. If you don't have data and if you don't understand the class of problem, or the opportunity, or the business process, or the end user, you have to collaborate or form a partnership of some kind. This idea of building something very early and getting feedback is key because the interaction that you get has value, plus you get the credibility of building and delivering something. I think starting with that incubation, even before you build, will change what you build or prototype, so begin by doing that.

I also think back to our principles. We made some very tough calls very early on. If you look at us today, we don't have any pharma investment, payor investment, or provider investment. We have never forked code,[13] so there's no custom code base. Because if you do that, you can't be a SaaS solution. We have purposely stayed away from creating conflicts of interest and perceived or actual favoritism. I can now honestly walk up to any oncology research or care provider and say, "I have no disclosures to make to you." I have nothing I've ever signed or done that creates a conflict for me. We decided that early on, and there were points in time that we had parties who would have liked to invest. Needless to say, it was a spirited conversation with the board about this. We told the board that we couldn't take the short-term view on this, because pivoting back from that doesn't actually work very well. There are some foundational things that define you and your company. However, defining your company is not just about the visuals you put together to describe what you're doing, nor is it about your pitch deck. There are other things, like who you take funding from, that define you.

> ***[W]e developed an attitude of knowing that different folks will choose to be here for different parts of our journey.***

The final thing is just people. I must tell you, it's a horror. Our startup team was great. But what I've learned is that different people who have domain expertise have different skills at different points in the life of the company, and so we developed an attitude of knowing that different folks will choose to be here for different parts of our journey. Now we refer to them as an alumni network because we don't want anybody to feel like not being here is a comment on anybody's worth. It's more a comment on where we are in our own journey in the company and things of that nature. So, we've tried to stay in touch with our alumni. In fact, we've had our first returnees of people who went off and then came back. It's super fun, actually, to see them coming back as different people because they now have different experiences, which is cool. But I think knowing how to manage the talent part is hard and important. And it's not just, "Ok, here's our group, so this is the group," without intervention. Your team is as strategic as some of the other aspects of the business that you're putting together.

But I'd like to reiterate that drenching yourself in the customer's market and getting feedback – you can't possibly overdo that.

[Author's note: We were about to sign off and complete the interview when the subject of regulatory approval came up. Here is the conversation we had.]

4.4.1 Regulatory Factors

We exist in multiple regulatory areas, following HHS and HIPAA for personal health information. But we also are part of running clinical trials, so we must follow FDA study subject rules, 21 CFR part 11, and other things that also come from HHS FDA. We have things that are medical device classification, so it's under software as a medical device[14] with 510(k) approval; we're actually a medical device manufacturer.

As a company, we've passed through regulatory-to-regulatory domain. We knew from the beginning, and we hired people into the company who had that background from the beginning. So, we designed for regulatory fitness from day 1, including putting SOPs [Standard Operating Procedures] and other processes in place. All of those early contracts actually called out regulatory fitness. If we didn't have the processes implemented, they had a [spending] cap or corrective action plan, with dates to meet those regulatory obligations.

Not only did we have to deliver what we said to initiate revenue, but also, as a company, we had to represent that we had a complete internal infrastructure and apparatus that allowed our customers to use our solutions for the intended use. And so again, there are different ways to think about your business architecture, cloud architectures, product architecture, business processes, and regulatory architecture.

Everything can also be thought of in terms of its phases, and we always work in three phases.

- Phase one – what we're building and delivering now
- Phase two – what we plan to build six to 12 months out
- Phase three – what we plan to build 18–36 months out

By setting up these three horizons, we are able to build the product keeping the next phase in mind. This allows us to deliver on the road map while maintaining the release sequence for the current phase. That's proven to work very well, because it keeps your thought processes focused because if you know where you're going to be at the end of the second phase, going into the third, it changes how you build in the current phase, too.

4.5 Notes

____

____

____

____

____

____

Endnotes

1 https://www.concertai.com/concertai-about-us/
2 https://my.pitchbook.com/profile/169832-62/company/profile#insights
3 More on ASCO https://asco.org/
4 More on CancerLinQ Building CancerLinQ for the Future: The Ne https://connection.asco.org/do/building-cancerlinq-future-next-step-ambitious-asco-projectxt Step for an Ambitious ASCO Project | ASCO Connection
5 More on BAAs https://www.hhs.gov/hipaa/for-professionals/covered-entities/sample-business-associate-agreement-provisions/index.html
6 More on BAAs https://www.hhs.gov/hipaa/for-professionals/covered-entities/sample-business-associate-agreement-provisions/index.html
7 More on QOPI https://society.asco.org/practice-patients/quality-improvement/quality-programs/qopi-certification-program/about-qopi
8 More on OncoEMR https://flatiron.com/oncology/oncology-ehr
9 https://www.mckesson.com/about-mckesson/newsroom/press-releases/2020/mckesson-launches-ontada-oncology-technology-insights-business/
10 More on federated architectures https://www.geeksforgeeks.org/federated-architecture-system-design/
11 Natural language processing-optimized case selection for real-world evidence studies. | Journal of Clinical Oncology.
12 More on CARA https://www.concertai.com/news/2024/01/concertai-highlights-2024-partnerships-strategy-business-results-and-ai-roadmap-at-42nd-annual-j-p-morgan-healthcare-conference
13 More on forked code https://www.codecademy.com/resources/docs/git/fork
14 More on software as a medical device https://www.fda.gov/medical-devices/digital-health-center-excellence/software-medical-device-samd

Chapter 5

DispatchHealth

They [Angel Investors] knew us as clinicians, as well as operators, and knew they could trust us and that we were going to work hard.

Kevin Riddleberger, Co-founder

5.1 Quick Facts

Website	https://dispatchhealth.com/
Founded	2013
Mission	*We deliver trusted, compassionate care in the comfort of home.*[1]
Founders	Kevin Riddleberger https://www.linkedin.com/in/kevinriddleberger/ Mark Prather, MD https://www.linkedin.com/in/markprathermd/
Unicorn status achieved	March 2021[2]
Funding rounds[3]	Seven funding deals • August 2015–November 2022 • Range from \$3.6 million in seed to \$330 million E round

DOI: 10.4324/9781032711034-5

Leading funders from Series E round[4]	• Optum Ventures • SVB Financial Group • Spark Growth Ventures

5.2 TLDR

Ideate

- Founded in 2013 under the name True North Health Navigation
- Focus on community paramedicine and sustainable business models
- Initial partnership with South Metro Fire Rescue to pilot community paramedicine
- Aim to reduce unnecessary utilization of 911 and ER services
- Leverage Medicare and Medicaid codes for billing services rendered on scene

Build

- Developed clinical protocols and technology capabilities
- Secured first payer contracts with Medicare Advantage and commercial plans
- Hired a branding agency and rebranded to DispatchHealth in 2015
- Built a call center and technology-driven standardized screening protocols integrated into a sophisticated logistics platform, which is patent pending
- Focus on high medical need, high social need patients

Launch

- Launched DispatchHealth on August 17, 2015
- Initial focus on senior living communities and private practice partnerships
- Expanded to Colorado Springs in early 2017 to build a playbook for new markets
- First out-of-state expansion to Phoenix, Arizona, targeting the senior population
- Secured first out-of-state health system partnership with Bon Secours Health System in Richmond, Virginia, in 2017

Grow

- Expanded clinical services to include post-acute transitional care and hospital-at-home
- Acquired two large portable imaging companies to control end-to-end service delivery
- Achieved national arrangements with United Healthcare, Humana, and others
- Continued vertical integration to deliver comprehensive care in the home
- Focus on delivering value-based care and managing high-risk patients

5.3 Meet the Founder

Kevin Riddleberger

Kevin Riddleberger, PA-C, MBA, is a seasoned healthcare executive devoted to reconstructing our nation's ailing and scattered healthcare delivery infrastructure into a more viable model. Boasting nearly two decades of hands-on patient care as a physician assistant and managerial expertise in healthcare, he is deeply committed to revolutionizing the way healthcare is delivered, focusing on technological innovation, procedural enhancements, and quality upgrades. Before co-founding DispatchHealth and taking on the role of Chief Strategy Officer, Kevin led the clinical solutions and strategic planning division at iTriage, a pioneering company in the consumer mobile health app sector.

A sought-after speaker at national events, Kevin actively engages in shaping legislative policies and is a recognized voice in influential publications like Authority Magazine, STAT, and Market Watch. In 2023, his efforts earned him the prestigious Leader of the Year award from the Colorado Academy of Physician Assistants. This honor underlines his substantial contributions to the medical profession, inspirational role amongst peers and patients, excellent leadership traits, commitment to high-quality healthcare delivery, and active involvement in community and voluntary endeavors. Kevin recently joined the board of directors for the American Academy of Home Care Medicine.

Educationally, Kevin holds an MBA specializing in healthcare administration from the University of Colorado at Denver. He earned his Master of Science degree from Rosalind Franklin University of Medicine and Science in Chicago, Illinois, and completed his undergraduate studies at the State University of New York at Plattsburgh.

Kevin Riddleberger is a visionary healthcare entrepreneur who fuses frontline clinical insight with tech-forward strategy. With more than two decades of experience as a physician associate, executive, and founder, he is driven to re-engineer care delivery through innovation, smart processes, and uncompromising quality.

As co-founder of DispatchHealth, Kevin recognized early the power of bringing hospital-level care into the home. Under his leadership, the company grew from a single-market pilot to the nation's largest high-acuity home-care network – 50 markets across 30 states – while saving payers and health systems $1.5 billion in documented medical costs. He architected DispatchHealth's omni-channel platform that unites patient engagement, clinical logistics, and predictive analytics, securing multiple patents for home-based acute-care technology.

Before DispatchHealth, Kevin led Clinical Solutions & Strategic Planning at iTriage, one of the first consumer mobile-health pioneers acquired by Aetna, honing the blend of clinical rigor and digital scale that defines his work today.

Kevin now serves on the boards of Medoma – Europe's leading care-orchestration platform – and the American Academy of Home Care Medicine, championing value-based, patient-centered models worldwide. He is a trusted advisor to startups across the country, pushing the boundaries of technology-enabled care delivery to achieve the quintuple aim.

A regular speaker at HIMSS, J.P. Morgan Healthcare, CES, and AARP Innovation Labs, Kevin inspires audiences to rethink where – and how – care happens. Whether mentoring founders or guiding boards, he unites clinical, operational, and financial stakeholders around a single vision: healthcare that is more accessible, affordable, and humane.

Kevin lives in Boulder, Colorado, with his wife – a fellow clinician – and is the proud father of teenage twins.

5.4 Interview with Kevin Riddleberger, Co-founder and Executive Advisor

The origin story dates back to 2013, when we officially incorporated under the name True North Health Navigation. We had the opportunity to partner with an EMS agency in South Denver called South Metro Fire Rescue. We put together a pilot for Community Paramedicine. (Community paramedicine is a relatively new and evolving healthcare model. It allows paramedics and emergency medical technicians to operate in expanded roles by assisting with public health and primary healthcare, and preventive services to underserved populations in the community. The goals are to improve access to care and to avoid duplicating existing services.)[5] From 2011 to 2013, there were many community paramedicine pilots that were successful based on grant money, but they didn't have a sustainable business model.

South Metro Fire Rescue had the desire to build a sustainable business model, thinking about it in a slightly different way. And so, Dr. Mark Prather, my co-founder, had an existing relationship with South Metro Fire Rescue as a medical director who helped establish this innovative public/private partnership to disrupt the status quo. We wanted to put an advanced practice nurse practitioner or a PA in the vehicle with the community paramedic, and leverage Medicare house call codes to help drive down unnecessary ambulance transports. We also wanted to be able to bill for the services that we were rendering on the scene, versus just operating on grant money.

> ***That was our idea for a sustainable model, and we really didn't know if it would be a sustainable model.***

That was our idea for a sustainable model, and we really didn't know if it would be a sustainable model. We knew it was going to be valuable. All the research was related to unnecessary utilization of the 911 system and unnecessary utilization of the ER. We knew the stats around utilization: 17% of 911 calls don't need to go through 911; 37% to 70% of patients, depending on which statistic or population you're looking at, don't need to be in the emergency department. And when you stack those costs together, $2,000 for an ER trip and $1,000 for an ambulance trip – if you're able to keep them at home, you're able to save a lot of money quickly.

We knew that we were going to drive value if we were able to keep those individuals in the home. We just didn't know how patients would perceive being able to receive this care in the home. We also didn't really understand the scope of clinical services that we could provide. We had to look at different technologies and then start to build clinical protocols from that. That's really where we got our start, demonstrated early success, and started to build confidence in the opportunity to build something transformational in the industry.

It was a boot-strapped pilot project on the side while I was still working at a company called iTriage, a consumer-facing mobile health app company that got acquired by Aetna. That is when I met Mark. I brought him onto iTriage to help me out with the development of our symptom processor and clinical content creation, and that's when we got talking about this concept more seriously around the opportunity to scale high-acuity care in the home. We started that pilot in September 2013. About a year later, we saw about 300 patients through that 911 service integration and structured our first couple of payer contracts with Medicare Advantage and commercial plans in the state of Colorado. We were able to share critical clinical and operational data from the EMST pilot with them, tracking every individual in terms of the outcomes 30/60/90 days after we treated them, impacting downstream utilization of ER and hospital services along with improved care coordination, using the state-based health information exchange called CORHIO.

> ***We wanted to be certain that the patients were staying out of the ER and actually saving money for payers.***

It was important to be able to track return to the ER within that 30/60/90 timeframe because we wanted to make sure that we weren't just treating patients episodically or in a fragmented way but connecting the patient to the patient's PCP or specialist to avoid the patient falling through the cracks. We wanted to be certain that the patients were staying out of the ER and actually saving money for payers. We also started to understand the potential challenges of scaling that model in the EMS world. We began having a lot of discussions with different individuals to develop a way that we could still operate in that model but pivot slightly, where individuals could contact us directly to be able to receive that same level of care in the comfort of their home, further upstream than the 911 system. We started to work on the refined clinical and operational model from Q3/Q4 of 2014 all the way up to the middle of 2015 to refine the concept, which required our first seed round of capital.

Here's a little fun nugget that helped us get on the national scene as we worked on our expanded clinical and operational model. Before we even launched with the expanded model, I was part of many different digital health/healthcare innovation think tank groups while still in my role at iTriage. As we were looking to secure our first office space for DispatchHealth, I got a random call from a NYC phone number, which I usually will not answer, but I did, and it was a reporter from the *Wall Street Journal* who was contacting me about a group I was part of, and then I proceeded to use the opportunity to pitch her on the concept we were building with DispatchHealth.

We were exactly at the right place at the right time to be able to raise capital, launch, and rebrand this new service.

Unbeknownst to me, with a little founder "luck," she was running a story about the early development of business models that were being labeled, "Uber for Healthcare." It was real serendipity. The WSJ ran the story, including DispatchHealth, while we scrambled to launch our new name, branding, and website to learn more about what we had built and were building for the future. We had this incredible media moment, and that's what really helped kick us off. There were a couple of other companies doing this at the same time, Pager and Heal, and they were highlighted in that two-page WSJ story as well. We then officially closed on our $3.6 million in seed funding to help us get launched and get our first vehicle outside the 911 system in Denver, Colorado. We were exactly at the right place at the right time to be able to raise capital, launch, and rebrand this new service.

So, we officially launched as DispatchHealth on August 17, 2015.

Sometimes you just need to take chances to make a difference.

And yet, to leave iTriage formally at the end of 2014 was a big leap of faith without salary to take a chance on truly transforming healthcare. I knew that we were delivering a lot of value at that time, and it was perfectly aligned with delivering on the Triple Aim. I got the green light from my wife, who is also a clinician, in terms of support, which is always important to have a supportive network behind you whenever you make big decisions in life.

But it was still a leap of faith. Sometimes you just need to take chances to make a difference.

> ***Many of the investors were telling us that the business model didn't make a ton of sense, because we were going to see less patients in each given shift.***

For the seed round, we included strategic individuals, as it was more of a friends and family round. We had some early investors who had been successful at building, scaling, and selling businesses in the past. Some of those individuals were partners at VCs, but they invested individually because they believed in us. They knew us as clinicians as well as individuals and knew they could trust us and that we were going to work hard on fulfilling our big transformational vision. That was probably the most important because at that time, we didn't have all the answers. Many of the investors were telling us that the business model didn't make a ton of sense because we were going to see fewer patients in each given shift. We were driving to see patients, so the efficiency was going to go way down compared to a traditional urgent care or ER or an office setting. So, the question was, "Why are you going to do that and why should we invest?"

But we had a lot of trust in where healthcare was going at that point. Due to the transition from fee-for-service to value-based care, we needed to remove costs from the system. We knew that the utilization of these large brick-and-mortar facilities was driving costs significantly.

> ***Any venture that is looking for seed money or even Series A should remember that the investors are really investing in the people and the potential.***

Like I said before, it was still a leap of faith. Any venture that is looking for seed money or even Series A should remember that the investors are really investing in the people and the potential; it's less about having all the answers at that point.

We continued to operate the EMS model with South Metro Fire Rescue when we launched. We applied a lot of the learnings that we had in that EMS 911 pilot over the course of the 18 months of running the proof-of-concept pilot, but there were a lot of things that we needed to build and to reconstruct with the vision of delivering on a tech-enabled service from the ground up. There was no off-the-shelf technology stack or playbook for what we were building.

We brought in trusted and talented software developers whom we had worked with previously at iTriage to help build the technology to support our approach. Previously, we had been leveraging the 911 system, and we needed our own infrastructure. We had to build a call center with integrated screening protocols, which was then integrated with a sophisticated logistics platform, which was then integrated into our EMR. This was not something we built overnight, so there was lots of manual work from the beginning, such as myself personally answering calls seven days a week, writing notes on little notepads, and then deploying the teams safely out to patients to take care of them. The benefit of owning the service and technology is that we could shape everything ourselves to fit our needs and use cases. All the technology we built out resulted in a patent-pending technology allowing for right-sizing, high-acuity care in the home.

Our mantra, from early days till now, has always been to focus on high medical need and high social need patients to drive the most value back into the system itself.

Our clinical experience also helped us understand how we needed to operate; how to build a quality system; how to ensure that we're following all the compliance rules; and how to chart, bill, and code from a payer perspective, resulting in value to the patient, provider partner, and payer. We needed to be extremely diligent to make sure that we were identifying the right patients from a health equity standpoint. Our mantra, from early days till now, has always been to focus on high medical need and high social need patients to drive the most value back into the system itself. That's been the foundation that we've built on: great experience and clinical quality outcomes resulting in value-driven care. And that's how we started to build the solution, focused on patients that we could safely remove from the ER system. Early on, we knew the clinical model worked well based on our early clinical encounters and data analysis, but it was critical to build the right technology in the right sequence to help us achieve scale and achieve the unit economics we forecasted. Lots of big questions early on to make the model work, to apply technology effectively. Lots of early questions on how to get this right. And how do we minimize the human element to be able to screen these individuals and help guide folks through that screening process safely?

The second big piece of this was, how do we move our teams efficiently from one location to another? We looked broadly to see if there was a healthcare logistics company or platform that we could use. There was nothing built that we could take off the shelf. We realized that we had an opportunity to build a moat around us. This would be our competitive advantage, giving us an early lead. By building a healthcare logistics platform, we were able to support this type of care delivery in the home. We were unique because we were responding to on-demand, unscheduled patient needs.

In the early days, we found ourselves waking up in the morning with no one on the schedule. We had no idea who would be calling us for help. Regardless, we needed to be able to fit them in and provide an efficient team to take care of them throughout the day. What we hadn't quite figured out was how the patients were going to remember to call us. How would they remember to use the mobile app when they're sick or injured and want someone to come to them? To avoid this initial issue, we began working in the senior living and home health industry. In these independent living and assisted living communities, the residents and staff were trained: when in doubt, call 911. These were the groups that were calling the 911 system, and they could easily see the value in avoiding taking a resident to the ER. We integrated our services with these early partners in their clinical protocols, where we had payer contracts in Colorado.

> ***Over time we began to segment customers into three different categories: senior care (senior living, skilled and non-skilled home health providers) health system; and strategic payvider partners.***

Our second target market was to work with colleagues that we had worked with who had their own private or specialty clinical practice or were affiliated with health systems that we had worked with previously. Many of these clinicians would get calls from patients, and their only option was to send them to the ER. But then the practitioners wouldn't know what was happening to their patients, resulting in fragmented, costly care and usually poor clinical outcomes. We decided to go out and train the clinicians and staff at these clinical practices, talking to them about our service and how to start using it as an extension of their practice, which allowed for some early product-market fit in this segment as well. Over time, we began to segment customers into three different categories: senior care (senior living, skilled and non-skilled home health providers), health systems, and strategic payvider partners. Strategic partners were typically individuals with value-based arrangements. As a small operating group, we had to keep all the plates spinning at once. At that time, we put more focus on the senior communities, home health agencies, and strategic partners. So that's where our focus was to start; we hadn't even touched the direct-to-consumer segment yet. We played with it a bit, but we knew we didn't have the expertise to pursue it and knew it could be extremely expensive without the right tactics. We knew where we could leverage existing trust with primary care groups, senior communities, and home health agencies. We established a pharmaceutical sales type of model, operating like drug reps. A group of us were going out, meeting with partners daily, and spending a ton of time knocking on doors.

Early in 2017, we had enough courage to expand to Colorado Springs, a couple of hours south of us. We decided that was the best thing to build – a playbook to open new markets. Even though it was a couple of hours south, it still allowed us to figure out the new model and answer key questions to perfect a playbook that was a short drive away. How would we order supplies and manage our supply chain? What would the office space look like? How would we manage different teams? What groups do we contact from a business development perspective?

At that time, the board was really pushing us to expand outside of the state of Colorado. We didn't know we were ready, but we went for it and decided to expand to Phoenix, AZ. We picked Phoenix because of the senior population there. We also had the opportunity to deliver the same value and leverage some of the payer arrangements and relationships in AZ that we had in CO, which was another big value add.

Our third expansion was to Virginia. In early 2017, there was a Becker's Hospital Review article that highlighted the 30 most disruptive companies, and we were highlighted in that article. We were just listed with our name and a few details. The CEO of Bon Secours Health System in Richmond, VA [Toni R. Ardabell], saw that list and really liked what we were doing. She was a big believer in moving toward value and care delivery in the home. She called us and asked us if we would come to Richmond, VA, and work with the Bon Secours Health System. We actually had to look up Richmond, VA, on a map, but it turned into an amazing partnership. We launched there in the latter half of 2017, making Bon Secours our second health system partner out of the gate. Toni was an amazing leader, forward-thinking, and an early adopter in moving care in the home. Now she is with Inova Health System, and we have a strong relationship there as well.

It was at that point that things really started to move forward quickly. But because every state is a bit different in terms of regulations and what can be done inside the home – what a PA can do, what a nurse practitioner can do – we had to plan and respond to variances from state to state. From a regulatory standpoint, that was key. We spent a lot of time and money on making sure that we were staffing correctly and delivering the right model of care in the particular state. Once we knew the process and regulatory constraints, we had what we needed to be able to hire the right individuals and identify the right profile to recruit.

Honestly, those early clinicians joined because they believed in what we were doing; they believed in the concept that, as a clinician, their focus should be to take care of patients, to be able to spend 40 minutes with their patients, and to sit next to the patient on the patient's couch in the patient's own environment.

But we were still a small company, a startup, and people took a chance by coming on board. Honestly, those early clinicians joined because they believed in what we were doing; they believed in the concept that, as a clinician, their focus should be to take care of patients, to be able to spend 40 minutes with their patients, and to sit next to the patient on the patient's couch in the patient's own environment. Our clinicians became invigorated and excited about delivering care in the home while getting out of the trenches of the emergency department. We tried to attract individuals who had great experience in the ER or urgent care setting but were looking for something new.

To manage this from a regulatory perspective, we engaged with a regulatory legal practice, and we worked with one specific person [Bruce A. Johnson] for many years. Bruce eventually came on as our office of general counsel because he was really excited about everything we were doing.

If I had to do it over again, would I have picked Phoenix as our first market to launch? I probably wouldn't have done it that way. We didn't have a great understanding of the market landscape. And healthcare is local. When you are an outsider coming in, it can be really challenging. We weren't aware of the dynamics of the Phoenix, AZ market, and there were a lot of home-based primary care groups. It was difficult. It was very, very difficult to start and get us going in that market. We could have picked a different market to expand into and have more success. But we are now better off having gone through those issues in that market.

> ***Being selected and deeply integrated by large health systems and/or payviders has become very important for us and it's still really important today as we expand into new markets.***

It's important to note that we selected Phoenix, and Richmond selected us, giving us a ready customer in Bon Secours. Being selected and deeply integrated by large health systems and/or payviders has become very important for us, and it's still really important today as we expand into new markets. You will not see us open a new market without a strategic partner. It's way too costly from a customer acquisition standpoint. We will always have an anchor partner when we launch new markets. It's much more fruitful to integrate with health systems service lines or work with a payer who has a lot of at-risk lives to manage, because we are well-aligned with our customers on what we are all trying to achieve – improved access to quality care while reducing costs. Experiencing the difference between opening those two markets generated a lot of learnings.

> ***Sometimes with successful companies, it's really about the right timing and some luck.***

After a couple of years of growth in many states, continued capital raises, and expansion of our clinical models, we, along with society, were hit with the COVID-19 pandemic. Sometimes with successful companies, it's really about the right timing and some luck. By the time COVID-19 hit, we had already scaled to states across the country. During COVID-19, our primary focus was to keep our providers safe as much as possible. We also knew that consumers were not able to access care. But instead of focusing on COVID-19 patients, we focused on individuals with underlying chronic diseases with acute problems who couldn't get in to see providers.

We became the valve that providers could open. They could say, "Call DispatchHealth," or "We'll get in touch with DispatchHealth to go out and see you," versus the patient coming into the clinic, ER, or hospital. We were helping to support the healthcare systems and ERs that were overrun. We continued to provide the services to the communities that we were already working with, in addition to the patients who didn't know where to go, didn't trust the system, or were too scared. That's where we concentrated our efforts.

> ***But the blessing in all of this was that toward the end of COVID-19, people started to open their eyes to the value and benefit of receiving care or healthcare services in the home.***

But the blessing in all of this was that toward the end of COVID-19, people started to open their eyes to the value and benefit of receiving care or healthcare services in the home. That's when telehealth and a lot of other different clinical models started to be developed. Additionally, venture money started pouring into services inside the home. That lit a fire underneath us as well, in terms of growth and opportunities with payers and investors.

Today, we are typically contracted by a payer; we have national arrangements with United Healthcare, although we started with state-based contracts. Once we got to a level of scale, UHG went through their medical economic review on the value we were creating. Based on that review, they got behind the solution in a big way and developed the national arrangement that we have today. That national contract helped us scale a great deal, because they started pushing us to go faster too, because they knew we were delivering value. We are now contracted with Medicare Advantage plans, commercial plans, and Medicaid plans, and we are also Medicare providers and Medicaid providers.

I think it's worth mentioning that as we expanded across the country, we didn't want our ED service to become commoditized. We started to see look-alike provider groups starting to do the same thing. In response, we started to expand the clinical services that we were offering in the home. It started in 2017, when we built a post-acute, transitional care service, identifying high-risk patients who were coming out of the hospital that had a higher propensity for readmission. We started scheduling a visit 24 to 72 hours after they transitioned out to help bridge the patient back to the primary care physician and make sure they didn't fall through the cracks.

> ***In 2019, we decided to look at our data and determine if we had an opportunity to hospitalize patients in the home. The data showed that the 6% of patients that we were escalating appropriately to the local ER to receive a higher level of care resulted in 75% of those patients being hospitalized. So, the question we had was, what if we became a decentralized***

hospital to care for these higher acuity patients, delivering further value to payers?

In 2019, we decided to look at our data and determine if we had an opportunity to hospitalize patients in the home. The data showed that the 6% of patients that we were escalating appropriately to the local ER to receive a higher level of care resulted in 75% of those patients being hospitalized. So, the question we had was, what if we became a decentralized hospital to care for these higher acuity patients, delivering further value to payers? Keep in mind, this was pre-pandemic, before the CMS[6] waiver [for acute hospital care at home], but we knew Johns Hopkins was already doing this. There was a physician, Dr. Bruce Leff, at Johns Hopkins, who was really the father of the hospital-at-home approach. He joined our advisory board and consulted with JHU about an opportunity to deliver hospital at home. We began with our first couple of contracts in Denver with a Program of All-Inclusive Care for the Elderly program and a local medical plan, and we started delivering hospital-level care in the home in November 2019, pre-pandemic.

And then there was a bit of luck again because we were doing it before the pandemic, and we had enough experience under our belt to scale along with the right technology infrastructure to do so. We are now offering this service in 15 different markets, supporting the CMS waiver for different health systems along with contracting directly with payers in the local markets to deliver this service ourselves (home-to-home admission).

Additionally, about 20% of our patients required imaging studies, and we were either using other portable imaging companies to help us get those studies done for people in the home, or we were sending them to facilities to get imaging studies done. We were concerned about the service level that we were getting in terms of the timing. Therefore, we decided to either build this capability ourselves or acquire this capability. We ended up acquiring two large portable imaging companies at that time – the first in 2021 and the second in 2022. Now, we can control the end-to-end workflow for digital X-rays and ultrasounds, all inside the home.

Today, we have a platform for delivering a complete system of care inside the home setting. Essentially, we have built this vertical integration in different markets over time to drive more and more value for risk-bearing entities.

So, like any capital raise over the years, we enjoyed the Unicorn designation for about 2 hours.

Obviously, having success by reaching a Unicorn (>1 billion) valuation status is a big deal and an amazing accomplishment, but it's not really what drove us from the beginning. It wasn't a milestone that we set. Early on, and still, the driving force today is executing on the Triple Aim (lower cost, better experience, and improved clinical outcomes). We knew then and still know today that if we keep our focus on these elements, success will follow, driving more enterprise value to all of our shareholders. We keep the patient at the center of everything we do, and knowing that we have touched over one million patients since inception with our transformative care model is one of the most gratifying things for myself personally. After we reached Unicorn status, we also knew that we weren't done. This [$1 billion valuation] was just a number, and we still had to continue to execute to continue moving forward. So, like any capital raise over the years, we enjoyed the Unicorn designation for about two hours. Then it's right back to work, staying focused, and just continuing to execute and move forward.

As for guiding other digital health founders, I would say healthcare has so many opportunities to improve, to align with the Quintuple Aim[7] in the US healthcare system. As a founder, use that as a foundation to ask yourself, "Am I offering an improved experience? Am I improving quality? Am I improving access? Am I driving down costs?" I think that is step number 1, and making sure that your product, your solution, your idea, is meeting some of those foundational elements to improve healthcare.

I also think that if people don't have a lot of experience in healthcare, they need to know it's a new world. It's a highly, highly regulated industry and a very complicated industry. A lot of what we do in healthcare doesn't make sense to people outside the industry. But the addressable market is worth $4.2 trillion, so you see a lot of folks, whether it's Walmart or Amazon or Facebook or any large company, trying to get into the industry. They see it as a great opportunity, but it's very, very challenging.

> ***It's not about just the founders. It's about the team around the founders.***

The other important factor is building a talented team. It's not just about the founders. It's about the team around the founders. We had a good team, and they all believed in our mission, so we could work really closely together from the outset. We wouldn't be here without an all-star team. I owe a lot of credit to everyone who came along on that journey early on and gave us this opportunity. Bottom line: you must have a great team around you.

It's about 1% improvement, every day. If you can deliver on 1% improvement, if you can learn, fail fast, and move forward and just continue to execute – that's key.

Then it's about putting your head down and executing. I recently read *Atomic Habits*, which is one of my favorite books by James Clear. It's about a 1% improvement every day. If you can deliver on 1% improvement, if you can learn, fail fast, and move forward, and just continue to execute – that's key. We operated in 90-day increments and considered just looking at 90-day increments, building a plan, and executing that plan. If you just keep doing that over and over again, you'll look back and you'll say, "Wow, we just did a lot!" On the other hand, if you look too far ahead or if you start looking backward too much, you start losing your focus, taking your eye off the ball.

I think customer service is often not viewed as important as it should be.

Another area is customer service. I think customer service is often not viewed as important as it should be. Especially in healthcare, it's doing what's right for the patients and doing what's right for your clinical partners in the community. If you continue to do that, good things will happen, and people will continue to work with you and trust your service. It's all about delivering a really good product.

I also want to mention that from an investor standpoint, we had and still have an amazing group of investors and board members. We were very purposeful when selecting board members and investors. We are fortunate to have a great mixture of venture capital investors who have a lot of experience in tech-enabled services or digital health services. These individuals came to us with a ton of experience. Additionally, having strategic investors on our board as well has been tremendously helpful, including Optum Ventures, Humana, Blue Cross Blue Shield, and ECHO Ventures, to name a few. So that mixture has been extremely valuable for us during our journey. Finally, as a result of COVID-19, having an opportunity to deliver hospital-level care at scale will be looked at as one of the greatest "block buster drugs" of our lifetime, in my opinion.

And we're just scratching the surface! It's a very complicated clinical operational model, but there are a lot of opportunities to be able to right-size care in people's homes and get great clinical outcomes without having to build $2,000,000+ per-bed hospital towers at a high clip where it's really, really hard to make a dollar without driving healthcare costs higher.

We're still in the early innings of it, but I have a lot of faith in the opportunity. And that is actually part of our Unicorn story – we weren't just a one-trick pony. We had the opportunity to have significant vertical integration to deliver extreme value, as value-based contracts continue to grow across the ecosystem.

And we do watch our competitors like Medically Home, and we have great respect for them. I sit on the board of the American Academy of Home Care Medicine with its chief medical officer, Pippa Schulman. We know Raphael [Rakowski, co-founder], and we all talk a lot. There is a lot of mutual respect between the two organizations, and this is a big enough market that many players can play. We're cheering each other on and wishing each other great success!

[Endnote: DENVER and BOSTON, March 18, 2025 – DispatchHealth and Medically Home today announced they have entered into a definitive agreement to merge, creating the country's most comprehensive provider of advanced medical care at home. Once the deal closes, Medically Home will become part of DispatchHealth. The combined entity will extend care into the homes of patients across 50 major metropolitan areas in partnership with nearly 40 health systems, as well as most major health plans and value-based care entities.[8]]

5.5 Notes

Endnotes

1 About DispatchHealth | What We Do & How We Got Here | DispatchHealth.
2 DispatchHealth brings in $200M to scale up in-home medical care | Fierce Healthcare.
3 https://pitchbook.com/
4 https://pitchbook.com/
5 Community Paramedicine Overview – Rural Health Information Hub.
6 https://www.cms.gov/newsroom/press-releases/cms-announces-comprehensive-strategy-enhance-hospital-capacity-amid-covid-19-surge
7 Why the Quintuple Aim is key to transforming healthcare – Health Data Management https://www.healthdatamanagement.com/articles/why-the-quintuple-aim-is-key-to-transforming-healthcare
8 DispatchHealth and Medically Home to Merge, Increasing Access to Hospital-Level Care at Home for Americans | DispatchHealth https://www.dispatchhealth.com/dispatchhealth-and-medically-home-to-merge-increasing-access-to-hospital-level-care-at-home-for-americans/

Chapter 6

Element Biosciences

There was not enough access to [DNA sequencing] around the world to look at all these different regions and different races.

– Molly He, CEO, Co-founder and Board Member

6.1 Quick Facts

Website	https://www.elementbiosciences.com/
Founded	2017
Mission	*At Element Biosciences, our mission is to empower the scientific community with more freedom and flexibility to accelerate our collective impact on humanity.*[1]
Founders	Molly He, PhD https://www.linkedin.com/in/molly-he-2243731/ Michael Previte, PhD https://www.linkedin.com/in/michael-previte-6a3610242/ Matthew Kellinger, PhD https://www.linkedin.com/in/matthew-kellinger-91092520/
Unicorn status achieved	July 2024[2]

DOI: 10.4324/9781032711034-6

Funding rounds[3]	Five funding deals • September 2017–June 2024 • \$5 million–\$277 million
Notable funders	• Foresite Capital Management • Venrock • T. Rowe Price Group

6.2 TLDR

Ideate

- Founded by Molly He and co-founders Mike Pavity and Matthew Kellinger
- Focus on increasing access to DNA sequencing
- Aim to democratize gene sequencing for smaller labs
- Address the challenge of high costs and centralized sequencing
- Use innovative surface chemistry and sequencing technology

Build

- Raised $5 million in seed money
- Rented a small, cost-effective office and lab space
- Purchased used lab equipment to save costs
- Developed a new surface chemistry as the first technical element
- Focused on a multidisciplinary R&D team

Launch

- Raised Series A funding based on new surface chemistry
- Expanded team to more than 50 people by mid-2019
- Raised Series B funding in late 2019
- Launched product virtually on Pi Day, March 14, 2022
- Emphasized product launch at AGBT conference in June 2022

Grow

- Developed multiomics capabilities integrating genomics and proteomics
- Expanded customer base to academic core labs and biotech/pharma companies
- Implemented telemetry for instrument health monitoring
- Continued innovation with new product offerings
- Focus on reducing risk premium and increasing value

6.3 Meet the Founder

Molly He

Molly co-founded Element Biosciences and has served as Chief Executive Officer since its inception. She has more than 20 years of experience in technology innovation and management in the biotechnology and healthcare industries and has sponsored initiatives encompassing research and development, operations, and life cycle management.

Molly was previously a Venture Partner at Foresite Capital, investing in some of the most exciting and innovative companies in healthcare. Before then, she was Senior Director of Scientific Research at Illumina, responsible for Illumina's global protein reagent innovation and improvements, and for leading global scientific and technical teams. She and her team have won twice the Innovation Award, the highest award for innovations with significant revenue impact at Illumina.

Before Illumina, Molly was the Head of Protein Sciences at Pacific Biosciences, where she was responsible for protein reagent development for their single-molecule real-time sequencing chemistry. She also has years of experience in the pharmaceutical industry, focusing on the structure-based design of antibody and small-molecule drugs targeting cancer and immune diseases.

Molly holds a PhD from the University of California, Los Angeles, in protein biophysics. She is passionate about science and technology education and has been a proud coach for the California State Science Olympiad competition since 2013.

6.4 Interview with Molly He, CEO, Co-founder, and Board Member

Why did I start Element Biosciences? There are two parts to the answer. First, why did I decide to start something on my own? And second, why Element? What was so attractive about the Element concept that I wanted to start it myself? The first piece really has something to do with my personality. I like to explore new things. I get bored very easily, and I've worked in many different types of industries myself. I've been in academia, and then I went to pharma and drug discovery. Then I worked on genomic tools and did some investing. I knew that I was always going to get bored if I worked for a company or an entity where I couldn't make the ultimate decisions and generate a lot of impact. I've always been a bit entrepreneurial.

The interesting thing is that when I was cleaning out my garage a couple of months ago, I saw all these old documents from the very early days while working on my postdoc. I'd already begun thinking about starting this company. Then I saw similar notes from when I was in my first industry jobs, where I was still thinking, "[T]hat would be a good idea for a future startup company." So, I was always thinking about it, but I never really settled on what to work on. That's why I continued to work for different industries, gaining experience, because I never really settled on what to start until Element. I think Element is a result of long-term meditation on the topic, wanting to start something cool. Ultimately, it was a combination of the time and maturity that I felt I had at the time.

> ***But for genomics, it was becoming very clear that everybody should have access to having their DNA sequenced, to have a better understanding of how they may suffer from certain diseases, and how they could be treated with medication or by changing their lifestyle.***

I'm a person who always feels like I'm an underdog, and I always want to fight for underdogs. And as I experienced all these different industries, I started to realize there are pros and cons for each industry, and a lot of challenges for each industry. But for genomics, it was becoming very clear that everybody should have access to having their DNA sequenced to have a better understanding of how they may suffer from certain diseases and how they could be treated with medication or by changing their lifestyle.

Genomics information was not fully accessible, even though in the past decade, there had been progress. Already, the price of sequencing has gone down, but when you look at the entire database, roughly 86% of genomics information came from Western European people, according to the stats I saw. There was not enough access to [DNA sequencing] around the world to look at all these different regions and different races. So, that got me thinking, "Why is that not accessible even though the price of sequencing has gone down so significantly?"

So, in talking with our co-founders, we quickly realized that the current sequencing market is highly segmented. There are high-throughput sequencing machines, and also low-throughput and medium-throughput by the incumbent. But it turns out that the lowest-cost DNA sequencing is only available on extremely large, factory-scale sequencing machines. These machines are very costly, and not everybody has access to them. Plus, even if you have the capital to access that kind of instrument, it will require you to sequence a lot more samples to get economies of scale. Not many people have that, so it's very centralized. But maybe there could be access to these kinds of technologies at a more affordable cost. So, our goal at Element is to increase access to DNA sequencing, even to the smaller labs that do not have enough samples to run on the large sequencers or do not have enough money to buy such a large sequencer. That becomes an extremely challenging technical problem. We asked ourselves, "How do we do this, without the economies of scale?" I found this topic extremely exciting and knew that it would require a lot of innovation. And that's why we started the company.

> ***Even when we raised the $5 million in seed money, (which I'll speak more about later) we felt like we needed to spend it very carefully.***

When we started the company, it was really a great experience because we were so excited and positive, just looking forward to great days and making a huge impact. We didn't really think about all the challenges that we would run into. But, having said that, I grew up in a very remote place in China. As a result, I've always been capital efficient. We had three co-founders at that time, and I was the only one getting paid through my venture firm. My other two co-founders, Mike Previte and Matthew Kellinger, quit their private, cushy jobs because they wanted to do this. Because they were not getting paid, there was a sense of urgency to get money raised. At the same time, we wanted to be very conscious about how we were spending the money. Even when we raised the $5 million in seed money (which I'll speak more about later), we felt like we needed to spend it very carefully.

We rented a place in a very old facility, subleased a small room, maybe 1,200 square feet of office space, and then another 2,000 square feet of lab space. It was like a basement, and there was no air conditioning. There weren't even cable connections for networking because the building was so old. The space belonged to General Atomics, where they had studied nuclear fusion, so it was very well insulated, with no cell reception. We sublet one of their little labs and an office. In the first week, we bought portable Wi-Fi devices and put them near windows; otherwise, we wouldn't get a signal. We also bought all these used pieces of lab equipment because we felt like we needed to be very thrifty until we generated some real data and knew we were on the right path.

As we were getting things started, we learned a lot. Being thrifty resulted in us finding this place that cost very little. I don't think I could find that kind of rent anymore these days. But the lesson we learned is that we probably should have rented a slightly better place so we didn't have to deal with surprises, like no cell reception or Wi-Fi. And because there was also no air conditioning overnight, we would see condensation on our buffer bottle for the reagents, and that was not ideal for the assays. Also, the air in there was not clean. We would see bacteria or mold growing in our cell culture media. We had all kinds of stuff causing more problems for us.

I think the lesson learned is that it may not be the best thing to be frugal to such an extreme.

I think the lesson learned is that it may not be the best thing to be frugal to such an extreme. We probably would have been better off with getting space that was actually set up for this kind of lab work, even though we would have spent a bit more, because our time would have been better spent. I feel like we wasted a bit of time there.

This industry is extremely capital heavy and capital hungry. We didn't realize that until much later in the game.

This industry is extremely capital-heavy and capital-hungry. We didn't realize that until much later in the game. And we really didn't know we would have anything that people would buy. We started in late 2017, and it wasn't until early 2019 that we started to feel like, "Wow, we are finally onto something," and I'm confident we're going to make it work. Making a DNA sequencer from scratch is extremely complex. Today, I can tell you that our sequencer has more than 4,000 parts. And that's just the hardware. And then there's software and reagents attached to that, which makes it even more complex.

We were just so naïve; we followed our passion and tried to make things work. We rebuilt every single technical element from the ground up.

Going back to our first days, I think that old Chinese saying is correct: newborn calves are not afraid of tigers. We were just so naïve; we followed our passion and tried to make things work. We knew there was an incumbent dominating the market for so many years. For us to make something new and better, faster and more affordable, it was going to take a significant amount of work. We could not be incremental. We had to be ten times better. So, how do we do that? Basically, we deconstructed the entire sequencing platform, down to each individual technical element. And that's where the Element name comes from. We reinvented every single element from the ground up, using a first principles approach. We also knew that the first sequencer was invented 20 years ago, so there were a lot of technical advancements globally that we could tap into, which were not being used in the incumbent's sequencer. We rebuilt every single technical element from the ground up. We started with the surface chemistry because we knew that surface chemistry (sequencing is just a surface assay; it's a surface readout) was extremely important to ensure we had a very high signal-to-noise ratio for the system. That was the first element we built, and we had strong confidence in it relatively quickly. And it was the surface chemistry that kept us going, even though we didn't have all the other pieces. Those other pieces included sequencing chemistry, which is very key; other pieces of hardware; the engineering work; and rudimentary software.

> ***We couldn't build a product on it yet, but we knew we had something, even though it took us a long time.***

We were making progress, but not to the point that we were confident. The surface chemistry was an anchoring point for us. After operating for a year, in 2018, all we had to show the investors was our new surface chemistry – nothing else. But based on that, we were able to raise our Series A, and then with the Series A money, in early 2018, we nailed down the basics of our sequencing chemistry, even though it was very preliminary. We couldn't build a product on it yet, but we knew we had something, even though it took us a long time.

When we were raising our Series A round, it became clear that it was very important to find the right investors for our business and that our investors needed to understand that this would be a long process. This was not a quick turnaround. This was going to take years and years, and probably decades of investment. I'm very lucky that we were able to find these investors, because we were very particular. Those were good times for raising money, as we were able to nail down some great VC firms with experience in this field and an understanding that it would take a long time. They even knew the ups and downs of building a sequencer. One of our investors was Venrock, also a very early investor of Illumina (the incumbent that we were trying to challenge), and knew the game. That was very, very important. The second piece for us was when we talked to our board of investors about this one element; we had to prove that the new technical elements of our surface chemistry were superior, though we didn't have all the other pieces to be superior. It became clear that even if we didn't have all the other pieces figured out to make a product that was ten times better, we could still have a product; it just wasn't going to be an *amazing* product. It would be a good product or an OK product. We'd still have a product, but it wouldn't be the ideal case. When we presented this concept to them, they felt that there was a fallback position, and the team was credible as innovators on this first element and needed more time to innovate on the other elements. So that's why they gave us more money to continue – to support the development of the other elements.

> ***Even though we were a very small company, we were very multidisciplinary, and this was a source of excitement for me.***

By the time we started the Series B round, around 2019, we already had about 50 people in the company, with most of them being R&D folks. (We've always been very heavily weighted toward R&D in our team.) We had maybe one lab manager type of person, and then we outsourced other functions like financing and accounting for a while. We were still small and too small to have full-time G&A people with us. The R&D folks were very multidisciplinary, because building a DNA sequencer is also multidisciplinary, and that was another exciting part – getting to interact with very different people every day. We also had – and still do – all kinds of hardware engineers, including electrical, mechanical, and fluidics, plus all kinds of software engineers. Also, we had a variety of chemists, including organic, biochemistry, surface chemistry, and molecular biology. Even though we were a very small company, we were very multidisciplinary, and this was a source of excitement for me.

> ***It was hard finding the right talent, because we had been in stealth mode for a long time and didn't come out of stealth until after we raised the Series B funds.***

It was hard finding the right talent because we had been in stealth mode for a long time and didn't come out of stealth until after we raised the Series B funds. So, imagine this. We knew this was a highly competitive field, and there was a huge incumbent. We didn't want to get their attention before we had something to show for our efforts. Before Series B, as I mentioned, we probably had at least 50 people. It was very difficult to hire because we were still in stealth. Before we invited a potential candidate on-site, we had them sign an NDA. We couldn't really tell them much, and the company didn't have visibility or a brand, right? So, in the early days, we hired a lot of smart kids, fresh out of school. Some had earned their PhDs, and some were right out of undergrad. They were hungry, and they wanted to learn something new. And they weren't too choosy, thinking that they had to work at a company with an established brand. We were very lucky that we were able to hire these folks in the early days, and it's very gratifying that many of them remain with us even today. It is just so amazing to see how much they have grown in the past seven years.

Our Series B round was $110 million altogether, broken into two tranches. We raised about $80 million in the first Series B, and then, immediately, COVID-19 hit in early 2020. We were very worried that we didn't know what to expect. So, we decided to top it off with another $30 million tranche to prolong our runway. The $110 million was used for productization because, although we had the sequencing chemistry as well as the other elements working, it was still far from a robust and seamlessly running product in market.

I might be getting a little bit too technical when we talk about sequencing. But in the industry, we talk about how many DNA bases you can read at the same time, in a single shot. The market standard at that time was about 150 base pairs that could be read in a single shot. Our first sequencing chemistry was working in early 2019, but there were only five bases. We had a long way to go to get to 150, let alone 300. So, the Series B money was used to optimize and scale the system so that it could be faster and cheaper and very robust. We also used the money to start building the manufacturing team as well as build the manufacturing prototype. It was only after our Series C funding that we started commercialization. I think that was in 2021, at the peak of the market, so it was super easy for us to raise our C round. And that was a huge round; I think we raised more than $270 million. I believe it was $276 million from top-notch investors, and it was totally oversubscribed. We had to tell investors to come back next time. It was an easy time to raise money, but that money was used to recruit commercial people, build the commercial product, and build a field presence. We virtually launched our product in March 2022.

I think we launched the product in a very unique fashion. The first thing is that we had been in stealth mode for so long. After Series B, to make recruiting a bit easier, we issued a press release, but we were still very vague as to what we were doing. We basically said we were doing genomic analysis or something along those lines. We didn't even say DNA sequencing. Because of that, the market was not educated about what Element was doing, and the market didn't really know what product we were coming out with or the specs. I think after Series C, we became a little more vocal, and we finally said that we were doing DNA sequencing. We said that we were making the next-generation DNA sequencer and all that, but nobody knew how it was different.

> ***There was absolutely no information out there, so the market was completely uneducated about us.***

That was the first challenge when we went to launch the product. There was absolutely no information out there, so the market was completely uneducated about us. The second piece that made it unique was launching during the era of COVID-19. So, we couldn't launch the product in a large conference setting like people usually do, even though we had hoped to.

> ***We fully intended to launch that product, in person, at that conference in February 2022. But a month before the conference, we got notice that the conference was delayed until June due to COVID-19.***

In the genomics industry, there is a very famous conference called AGBT (https://www.agbt.org/). Everybody launches their new products there. We were so excited to launch our product, we actually paid for a very high level of sponsorship. I think we were a silver sponsor, which is a top sponsor. We fully intended to launch that product, in person, at that conference in February 2022. But a month before the conference, we got notice that the conference was delayed until June due to COVID-19. But we decided we didn't want to wait until June. The product launch already had its own timeline, and we were all geared up for it. People were excited. Internally, we were excited. We had such strong momentum. We asked ourselves, "What do we do?" Overnight, our executive team decided we wanted to do our own launch virtually. Obviously, we couldn't do it in February, as that was too close. We didn't have anything lined up for a successful virtual launch. So, we decided to be a bit geeky and launched on Pi Day, March 14, 2022, virtually, and then in June we went to the physical AGBT conference and launched again. That gave us two shots to get it right.

So, that was our decision about launching our product. I think that the team did an amazing job putting everything together very quickly. It was a very well-received launch. Everybody gave us an A+ rating.

Our virtual launch lasted about an hour and a half. We had pre-recorded executives speaking, and our early access customers speaking, plus testimonials from our partners. Then we had our own R&D team talking about the products, followed by 30 minutes of live Q&A with founders and executives. It was extremely well done.

At that point, the world knew what Element was about, what kind of product we had, and there was a lot of excitement. And then we went to the AGBT conference in person in June and amplified our message.

> ***We launched the product knowing that our product could do everything that the incumbent could do.***

We launched the product knowing that our product could do everything that the incumbent could do. We knew that we were not launching into a niche market. We wanted to be application agnostic, so we didn't really put a lot of restrictions or emphasis on particular market segments. We just let it go wild. So, when we started thinking about early adopters, we didn't know who would be adopting this sooner than others. We wanted to let the market tell us. Very interestingly, we saw a huge uptake, in relative terms, in the academic core lab facilities. These are the university labs that have many different types of instruments. They take examples for experiments from the individual PIs (principal investigators) and then return the results to them. That's what a core facility is. These organizations became our early adopters, which exactly fit our marketing thesis, our original vision. Their pain point in the past was that they couldn't go with a very high-throughput instrument; first, because the instrument is very expensive, and second, because they were required to run a lot of samples in a batch on that instrument. Their individual researchers always said they wanted the results quickly, like the next day or something. But they had to wait two to four weeks to get their results. The other option was to run on a low-throughput instrument. That would give them a faster turnaround time, but at a higher cost because it was so expensive to run only a few samples at a time. There were no economies of scale. Illumina charges were very expensive in terms of run costs. With our new instrument, labs can run a few samples at a time, but at the factory scale cost per sample. So essentially, they were able to get the best from both the retail world and the wholesale world, to use an analogy. And that was why they were so excited to have this instrument. They could keep the low cost as if they were running on the high-throughput instrument, but their turnaround times were a lot faster.

> ***We thought this is a such amazing product, because it's lower cost, much better quality than the incumbent, and very fast. So why wouldn't anybody buy it? It's like a no-brainer.***

Scaling from there was painfully slow because we were so naïve. We thought this was such an amazing product because it's lower cost, much better quality than the incumbent, and very fast. So why wouldn't anybody buy it? It's like a no-brainer. We were thinking, "Hey, we don't even need a salesperson. People will just come to buy." But it turns out it's completely the opposite. We had some early adopters, and they were happy with the instrument, but the scaling was slow because we underestimated the power of the incumbent. There was a perceived risk premium attached to our brand. It goes back to the saying, "Nobody gets fired for buying IBM," because it's a safe choice. You don't need to take a risk. Even though it's a little bit more expensive, it works, you're used to it, and the entire ecosystem was built for that incumbent. Whether it's data analysis or upstream sample prep, it was all built for that ecosystem, so penetrating that was very hard. I think we hit quite a few roadblocks because of risk premium issues. Overcoming that risk became our key focus. One thing that our product team did really well was to make sure that our workflow was completely compatible with what people were using, enabling us to play in Illumina's existing ecosystem. By making the data analysis and sample prep workflows compatible, we were able to minimize the switching cost to almost 0. That lowers the risk premium.

> ***We also hired our field service and support people even before we hired our salespeople.***

The second thing we did, which was very important in retrospect, was build a very robust instrument. As a newcomer, there was zero room for error. If the instrument wasn't robust in the field, if it broke down every week, then nobody was going to buy it anymore. So, it was very gratifying to see our engineering team, our chemistry team, and our manufacturing team do such a great job building a super robust box, which had gone through many, many in-house tests before we shipped it out. We also hired our field service and support people even before we hired our salespeople. We knew that it was going to be incredibly important for us to be able to support our instruments in the field flawlessly. So, that was the second piece to reducing risk premium.

> ***[I]t was a "try before you buy," kind of thing.***

The third piece was that a lot of customers wanted to see data with their own eyes. They didn't want to buy before they tried it. How could we solve that? We didn't want to give instruments away because these are very, very expensive instruments. We couldn't afford that. What we did instead was to start a very small service lab internally. The goal was not to make revenue but to basically take customer samples, run them internally, and return the results back to customers. That way they could analyze the samples themselves and compare them to their original data. That helped quite a bit in converting these customers into buying instruments – it was a "try before you buy" kind of thing. In the early days, we had a 50% conversion rate of these customers buying instruments, which is very high. But now that our brand has been de-risked, conversion rates have started to come down because people just buy the instrument. But in the early days, the service lab had its purpose. We effectively offered a service that replicated the experience they would have if they had bought the device. We still charge for the material at about $3,000 for one experiment. But people are willing to do that because $3,000 is a relatively small investment. And if they buy the instrument, we'll credit that money back to them most of the time.

> ***I think being a bit paranoid is good for the company, although I also think we are making an impact.***

But even with all of this, I will say something that you probably won't expect. I always think that we're not there yet. We're not out of the woods. I always have this healthy amount of paranoia. I think being a bit paranoid is good for the company, although I also think we are making an impact. We're making a change in the industry for the first time. The reason why I know is that Illumina is now cutting their price and undercutting us everywhere we go. I think they're taking us extremely seriously now instead of just dismissing us or brushing us aside. That is very telling to me – we have poked the bear, and we are real. I'm very proud of this. We finally made the bear move.

I'm so happy they're falling into the trap of discounting all day long to their huge install base. We're in the mid-throughput realm, and that's not their bread and butter. Their bread and butter is high throughput, so they can afford to undercut us on every single box and squeeze us out. And we know that. The important thing is to play chess, not checkers. Look multiple steps ahead, right?

> ***So, now we're at the point where they're competing with us on price, just as we're starting to compete with them on value.***

When we first built the instrument, we thought about going beyond DNA sequencing with the same instrument. That way, people could have a fully integrated system to understand not only genomics but also proteomics, the entirety of biology. This gave us differentiation that Illumina couldn't do. So, now we're at the point where they're competing with us on price, just as we're starting to compete with them on value. We can provide premium value because they cannot offer a fully integrated system. New products coming out on the same instrument really integrate genomics information with proteomics, even cell biology information. That changed the industry once again because we are now leading in the multiomics space, and this is where we can win.

There are new customers who want the multiomics products in addition to DNA sequencing. These are completely new customers for us, mostly in biotech and pharma, which is very exciting for us. And then there are also existing customers, for example, these core labs in academia who also want to have these new capabilities. They call and say, "Hey, I want to upgrade my instrument to have the multiomics capability." We now see a mix of customers using these new products, both existing customers and net-new customers that we did not have before.

But there's still a lot more to build. This is only the beginning of our product offering because I like to build things. It's almost like the gift keeps on giving. This is all about a first principles approach. When we first built this system, we wanted it to be future-proofed so we could keep on adding new things to the system. We're just getting started on multiomics. There's so much more we can do. And obviously, this is just one instrument. We have one platform, but we're not going to be a one-platform company. We will continue to build different platforms too, and that's for the future.

We're very happy that we made the right decision to go outside just sequencing alone. This was something embedded in our initial thinking, and it has proven out over time. Otherwise, we would not be able to sustain these kinds of pricing pressures. We are better at sequencing, but there are other options. And if people don't care how much money they spend, they can totally use other options. We're very happy that we insisted on the multiomics approach and making additional applications on the sequencer. This way, we can be fully differentiated.

> ***[W]e underestimated human psychology because buying is a very emotional process. Everybody wants to feel like they're winning something.***

One thing that we misjudged was the pricing strategy of our DNA sequencer, which ties into our naivety. We thought it was such a great instrument that everybody should just buy it. We also thought we would have transparent pricing. We wouldn't even need to negotiate price. We would just set the price, and people would buy at that price, right? That was our original approach, but we underestimated human psychology because buying is a very emotional process. Everybody wants to feel like they're winning something, so it's very hard in this industry to offer one single price. Everybody wants to bargain. Everybody wants to get the best deal they can. So, we started to loosen that up, depending on things like their sample volume. Depending on each individual's situation, we may give a discretionary discount, which is more of a normal sales practice.

> ***Every quarter we measure NPS (Net Promoter Score) and we're very happy that our NPS scores are extremely high.***

We also get feedback from customers on things other than price. We have many ways of getting feedback. There is spontaneous feedback given through our field application scientists and all that. Plus, we have a very structured survey format. Every quarter we measure NPS (Net Promoter Score), and we're very happy that our NPS scores are extremely high. We also see all these different comments from our customers.

But one thing that I do want to single out is the telemetry capability that we have on the instrument. Ninety percent of our customers' instruments are connected to our Element cloud. We don't see the actual data they have, but we do monitor the health of the instrument, how many days it's been running, and what problems they are running into. We collect this vast amount of information, and we use it for future improvements. So that's also super helpful.

> ***But I'm very happy to see Element is starting to make that impact, and that's why we founded this company.***

When we achieved Unicorn status, I think it had a lot more significance for our employees than for me. I never really thought twice about it. I never dwell on that kind of stuff. What's more important to me is that our employees eventually get what they deserve. They put in a lot of hard work, and if our valuation is high, I'm super excited about it because they are going to get the benefits from their hard work. The other piece that's really important to me is that Element, as a company, is really making an impact – improving society, improving healthcare, making a difference. I've seen many companies with good intentions, but eventually they don't make it. They don't make the impact they wanted to. But I'm very happy to see Element is starting to make that impact, and that's why we founded this company.

I think this is a unique company, and some ex-employees or current employees may not think of it as the best place to work because we have a very high bar for performance. But if people enjoy fast-paced innovation and open debate, and they won't shy away from that, they will enjoy Element more than other places and grow significantly in their career path. Element is not a fit for everybody. It's for risk takers. It's for passionate risk takers with a focus on the mission.

6.5 Notes

Endnotes

1 https://www.elementbiosciences.com/about
2 https://my.pitchbook.com/profile/223740-64/company/deals#deal-266646-97T
3 https://my.pitchbook.com/profile/223740-64/company/deals#deal-119810-80T

Chapter 7

Innovaccer

I think a lot of founders make the mistake of hiring people when they need them, when really, you have to hire a person that will fit into that role 2 years from now.

Abhinav Shashank, CEO and Co-founder

7.1 Quick Facts

Website	https://innovaccer.com/
Founded	2014
Mission	*Improve patient outcomes.* *Grow market share.* *Save providers time.* *All in one AI-enabled cloud.*[1]
Founders	Abhinav Shashank https://www.linkedin.com/in/abhinavshashank/ Kanav Hasija https://www.linkedin.com/in/kanavhasija/ Sandeep "Sandy" Gupta https://www.linkedin.com/in/9sandeepg/
Unicorn status achieved	February 2021[2]

DOI: 10.4324/9781032711034-7

Funding rounds[3]	Nine funding deals • July 2016–July 2024 • Range from \$15.6 million to \$20 million
Notable funders	• WestBridge Capital • Lightspeed Ventures • Mubadala Capital • B Capital Group • M12 • Kaiser Permanente

7.2 TLDR

Ideate

- Founded by Abhinav Shashank, Kanav Hasija, and Sandeep "Sandy" Gupta
- Initial focus on creating a common platform for data integration across industries
- Early success with Fortune 500 companies like Disney, Wolters Kluwer, and NASA
- Shifted focus to healthcare due to large scope and opportunity

Build

- Developed industry-specific data models for entertainment, publishing, aerodynamics, and healthcare
- Focused on healthcare with initial customer Mercy ACO
- Rapid growth through referrals and strong product credibility
- Hired CMO Dr. David Nace, who helped build an advisory board with industry leaders

Launch

- Launched care management product, including decision support, patient engagement, and customer relation management (CRM) system
- Expanded product offerings to 16 modules, with plans for hundreds more
- Leveraged a fixed data model for rapid innovation and product development
- Achieved HIPAA and HITRUST compliance for healthcare products

Grow

- Raised multiple funding rounds, including Series A through Series F
- Faced challenges with early ecosystem development, leading to a strategic shift
- Focused on long-term sustainability and organizational structure
- Emphasized the importance of culture and mentorship for growth

7.3 Meet the Founder

Abhinav Shashank

Abhinav Shashank is the CEO and co-founder of Innovaccer, a San Francisco-based healthcare AI company on a mission to revolutionize healthcare through intelligent, data-driven solutions. Committed to bringing joy back to the practice of medicine and patient care, Abhinav has emerged as a visionary strategist, driving transformative change across the healthcare landscape.

Under his leadership, Innovaccer has become a national leader in population health management and healthcare AI, earning more than 100 awards and over 300 analyst recognitions. His initiatives have helped save the US healthcare system $1.5 billion in cumulative costs and forged partnerships with over 150 healthcare organizations. These innovations propelled the company to a $3.2 billion valuation.

At the heart of Abhinav's vision is the belief that healthcare doesn't need to feel this hard. He is building a future where care is frictionless, where disconnected data becomes unified intelligence, burdensome workflows become effortless, and the entire care ecosystem operates as one.

Abhinav's thought leadership is equally influential, with over 300 published articles, and has been recognized in Modern Healthcare's 40 Under 40, Becker's Hospital Review's Rising Stars: Healthcare Leaders Under 40, Goldman Sachs' Most Exceptional Entrepreneurs of the Year, Fortune India 40 Under 40, and Forbes' 30 Under 30 Asia: Enterprise Tech.

He envisions a world where healthcare is 100% consumer-centric and value-driven, powered by AI, compassion, and the pursuit of truly frictionless care.

7.4 Interview with Abhinav Shashank, CEO and Co-founder

Our broad mission is to unlock healthcare data, and by doing that, we create joy of care for the patient, provider, and every stakeholder in the care delivery process. Given how large and complex the healthcare ecosystem has become, the human touch of healthcare has vanished a little bit. All of us are looking for healthcare that includes a human touch: that someone on the other end of the process cares and that we are going to be well taken care of.

In some way, this has been because of all the complexity that has been created. I think that by liberating the information and data, we end up creating tools and technologies that help rekindle the joy of care.

When we started the company, we were 24 or 25 years old and weren't thinking specifically about healthcare. Our broad thesis at that point was the fact that enterprises were going to be creating massive amounts of data, and there wasn't an integrated technology stack that existed, a system of intelligence. For example, Salesforce is the system of record for everyone in sales, right? There was no system of intelligence that existed from that perspective. Enterprises therefore ended up using five different things; they used ETL [extract, transform, and load] layers and separate tools, like Informatica. Then they would use a data warehousing layer, such as Snowflake or an Azure product, and then add a separate visualization layer and create an Application Programming Interface (API) on top of it. By the time all of this got stitched together, the project was probably already over budget, and no one really cared to figure out how to sort it out, and the initial intent of the project went away. Meanwhile, the problem still isn't solved.

So, that was our general intent: to create a common platform on which all these functionalities exist. We wanted to build everything from the ETL layer to warehousing, to visualization, to creating your own models, to opening it up as an API, and making it available for enterprises.

We decided to build it, not realizing how much work it would require. It took us about 18 months or so, I think, to stitch together something that was like an MVP. Then we went with our MVP to enterprises, and it seemed that our thesis worked out pretty well. We got Disney, Wolters Kluwer, NASA, and other Fortune 500 companies very interested in the platform. Everyone responded, OK, let's go solve this problem or that problem, and very quickly we ramped up to $5 million or so of ARR.

> ***Now, I think the thing we missed was that every industry needed its own data model. We had missed that fact in our broader thesis.***

Now, I think the thing we missed was that every industry needed its own data model. We had missed that fact in our broader thesis. If you create it as an agnostic tool, you can't keep replacing the data model everywhere. We created a data model for entertainment with Disney, a model for publishing with Wolters Kluwer, a model for aerodynamics with NASA, and a model for healthcare with Mercy [https://www.mercyone.org/]. It was too much for a startup to take on, and because we had to create specific data models for each industry, it took a lot of time and effort.

So, we decided that we were going to have to focus because at that point we were very clear that the product is needed in every industry, right? Healthcare seemed like the most underdeveloped in terms of technology adoption. Therefore, the scope and opportunity were very large, so we decided to focus on healthcare. We already had one healthcare customer, Mercy ACO, and they wanted to run on top of our platform, which gave us an insider's look. We were shocked by what we saw, thinking, "[T]his cannot be true – this cannot be how they are using these systems."

At that time, I had not gone to an American hospital for treatment ever, nor had I even been to a primary care doctor. So, we were approaching it from a very engineering- and technology-first approach, and I think it helped. Because we started thinking about everything in first principles, why was this working this way? We asked a lot of questions. I think our first deployment went really well because the customer scaled our work from $500(k) to a couple of million dollars. Then we scaled it to six other health systems within the first year, getting to approximately $8–9 million ARR. We went from $0 to say about $5 million in 24 months and up to about $10 million in the next 24 months.

> ***Our biggest sales driver has been referrals.***

What we realized was, if you have a good product in healthcare, you don't even need much of a sales team because everyone talks to each other. Our biggest sales driver has been referrals, when someone spoke to someone else and they said, "Oh, we used Innovaccer for this." Our initial sales team was the three or four of us – not even a real sales team. We just went and talked about the technology, and the customers on the other side of the table would just nod. Probably they weren't even getting what we were saying from a technology perspective, but someone had already given a reference, and I think that was what the customers were banking on. We typically spoke with CIOs, CMOs, chief medical information officers, and, in some cases, CEOs, too. Because we were a fairly young startup, people wanted to meet the founders before they engaged, and this was not a small or simple sale. If you're going to have your data infrastructure managed by someone, you really want to meet the founding team and make sure they're credible and they can deliver the platform.

Our product was really, really strong because we had already deployed our platform at Disney, at Wolters Kluwer, and other Fortune 500 companies. We had already gone through security processes and built out the features and processes that Fortune 500 companies would need. So, this data infrastructure product was not a new thing for us.

> ***We spent a lot of time curating references to make sure our customers could become evangelists for us, rather than us trying to aggressively sell.***

We also had expertise because we had worked with 65 of the top 100 research institutions, such as Harvard, MIT, and Stanford. We had been deploying this product for free for them and had earned a lot of credibility already, so we knew the data. We had references from the top 100 research schools, not healthcare research, but broadly. We had gotten a reputation for understanding data and things of that nature. We worked on the principle of references very strongly. We spent a lot of time curating references to make sure our customers could become evangelists for us, rather than us trying to aggressively sell.

Everyone wanted a data infrastructure, so there was a budget line item for one almost everywhere we went. And once the need was confirmed, our solution was one-third the cost of enterprise software companies, and even on that, we made about 80% gross margin. Because we were cloud-natively built and because we were built using a microservices architecture, it was easy to deploy, and the infrastructure costs were not too much for us.

Most of the companies that we were competing with in healthcare, at that point, were similar to McKesson, and those vendors had architectures from the previous technology generation, including on-prem. They had large software footprints with big deployments, and the cost was about three times ours. I also don't think they made an 80% margin, like we did, even though it was three times the cost.

It was a fairly clear decision for the CIO that the cost of our platform was lower. Additionally, the outcome seemed better, and we had references. But it wasn't always a slam dunk. If we pitched to 100 customers, we would probably end up working with five; five is a great outcome when you're selling $1,000,000 a year deals, right?

> ***Once we moved from Fortune 500 enterprises into healthcare, we hired our Chief Medical Officer, Dr. David Nace. We hired him right after we got our first healthcare customer.***

Once we moved from Fortune 500 enterprises into healthcare, we hired our CMO, Dr. David Nace. We hired him right after we got our first healthcare customer. Dr. Nace had worked at McKesson and had been the CMO at Aetna. He had lots of tech experience and was at MarkLogic when we hired him. He has been incredibly instrumental in our growth. He set up this advisory board for us, including Glenn Steele from Geisinger; Phil Fasano, who was the CIO of Kaiser and is currently Chairman and CEO of Recuro Health; Mark Ganz, the former CEO of Cambia Health Solutions; and Jonathan Bush, founder of athenahealth and currently founder and CEO of Zus Health. We didn't know these people, but Dr. Nace did, which was so helpful.

With Dr. Nace's help, we moved from selling an infrastructure to launching our care management product, which included a point-of-care decision support product, a patient engagement product, and a CRM product. It was all healthcare-specific and built after Dr. Nace arrived. Prior to that, the only thing that we had was this data infrastructure layer, which had a healthcare data model already built out.

Working with Mercy was also very helpful. We were already building a lot of products internally at that point, but working with Mercy informed our product road map. Within the first year, we got six more healthcare customers. And then additional customer needs started to surface, because they would ask things like, "Now that I have this data infrastructure, can you help us put population health analytics on top of it?" Once the dashboards were done, they would say, "OK, this is good, but I want my care managers to be able to use for their care protocols and stuff." So, we built out a care management product on top of it.

All of this is SaaS, so our customer could just add to their existing subscriptions, with each module having its own price. People may choose to take two of our modules or buy the entire suite, which now has 16 modules. Hopefully, at some point, there will be hundreds of modules for customers to purchase.

Our general thought process was that it's very easy to build software on a core data infrastructure where the data model is fixed. It would be very hard to do this, on something that doesn't have a fixed data model; half of the data resides in the core HR system, and half of it resides in claim systems, lab systems, and other systems. So, when you get all these things together and I can access one data element, now it's party time for developers, right?

We launched products so quickly; I don't think there are other companies that have launched 15 or 16 products in the same six to seven years, like we have.

We've been able to innovate quickly. Our CTO, Mike Sutten, says that people think business defines architecture, but his approach is that architecture defines businesses, especially in the technology space. I think we were just fortunate that we chose the right architecture, which continues to allow rapid innovation on top of it. If that architecture hadn't existed, it would have taken us a lot more time to build products. Now, most of the time it takes us to launch a product is actually in testing it.

Building new modules is the smallest quantum of time that we take. We can launch a product in two weeks from today if we decide to build today. We could put a scrum team on it and finish in about two weeks because there is a design system, there is a data model – everything already exists. We can launch a product in two weeks from today, but it's healthcare, right? So, we must test everything, and now our general release time for a new product is about eight to nine months to make sure that everything is HIPAA and HITRUST compliant.

When we were raising our seed round in 2014, we had no customers because we were still building the product. However, we had some proof because universities were already using it; university researchers were using our half-baked product. So, we asked them, "Would you pay for this?" It was essentially a test bed, and then we put a price tag on it, generating about $1.5 million in revenue. Our general view was that if universities can pay

$1.5 million, enterprises will certainly pay a lot more. So, that was our pitch to seed investors. I think we raised $3.5 million as a seed round, split into two tranches: roughly $1 million in the first and $2 million in the second tranche. That took us through the first two years, 2014 to late 2015. Then, at the end of 2015, we raised our $15 million Series A, led by WestBridge Capital and Lightspeed India. We were still based in India, traveling back and forth to the United States. At the time, it was India's largest Series A round. Of course, now people raise $15 million in seed and pre-seed rounds, but back in 2014, $15 million was real money!

A year and a half later, we raised our Series B. We were growing so fast, our investors told us that we didn't have to look for additional investors. Lightspeed and WestBridge funded our Series B round, too. And then Microsoft joined an extension, our B1 round, so to speak. Our growth was pretty good for the next year as well. Our Series C [Feb 2020] was funded by Tiger Global, Steadview, and Dragoneer. Then Series D [Feb 2021] was led by Tiger Global, and Mubadala joined. And then Series E [Dec 2021] was led by Mubadala, and Series F was led by Kaiser Permanente [May 2024].

Despite all the funding rounds, we did make a few missteps. As I said, our general thesis was that there is going to be a platform at some point, and we would open it up, and an ecosystem would be built on top of it. We started doing that when we were at about $40 million in ARR. But when you aren't that large, and you start investing in the ecosystem, it becomes clear that you've started this process too early. Salesforce started their ecosystem when they were about $500 million. We tried building our ecosystem super early, and the result was that we did OK, but it wasn't a revenue generator. We would have other startups coming and building on top of our platform, but it felt like such a waste because there was no real revenue.

> ***What we realized was that, if you're not of significant size and scale yourself, creating an ecosystem on top of your platform is very expensive and potentially can kill you.***

We realized that it took a lot of effort and energy to build an ecosystem. It took so much capital to create. Even though we went from $40 million to $70 million in ARR, which was great from a PR perspective, we burned $70 million trying to make it work. We had just completed a funding round with a $3 billion valuation while burning through $70 million. Suddenly, everyone is asking, "Where are the profits?" So, we had to shut down our entire ecosystem with the plan to restart it at some point. What we realized was that, if you're not of significant size and scale yourself, creating an ecosystem on top of your platform is very expensive and potentially can kill you. Once we shut down the entire initiative, our burn rate decreased from 100% a year to become profitable in about 18 months.

It sounds easy on the surface, right? But making a transition from that mode to a more focused approach sparked organizational upheaval. People were emotionally invested in setting up the ecosystem, and now suddenly we had to rein all of that back in. And then we had to rebuild momentum in one particular direction. It was very, very hard to do organizationally, for sure. We had to let go of about 20% of our team of 1,400 people. It was very, very hard, and this was the first time I had done this. I was still only 33 or 34 years old. And because I like to take a very active role in hiring, I had hired a lot of these people and had to let them go. Some of them had left big Silicon Valley jobs, and then it didn't work out, and it was horrible. I went into, like, a year-long depression after that, where I was clinically diagnosed with depression. I went to the board and told them I needed a four-month sabbatical. I took off to India and went to a lot of different places; it was just too much for me emotionally. The business was doing well; that wasn't the challenge. But it was very emotional for me. My daughter was maybe six months old; we had moved into a new home, and now I had to do a bunch of layoffs.

If I were to advise people on how to start a company, I would say, "Don't! It's harder than you think."

We've been on the path of hiring some of those people back as we can, if they want to come back. But now we're three times the size we were at that time. I think my learning from that experience is that there are false starts, and some of them are massive. People talk about entrepreneurship and say, "It's so fun and great." But it's really hard. If I were to advise people on how to start a company, I would say, "Don't! It's harder than you think."

We were initially on AWS only, and then Microsoft invested, and we got early access to a lot of Microsoft products. I also met Satya [Nadella] a couple of times and saw how healthcare was a strategic priority for the company. Microsoft wanted to partner, and it seemed like Microsoft was very invested in the success of companies in the healthcare space. So, now we run on both AWS and Azure.

The technology was the foundation for our name. Ovation Accelerator was our initial idea for the company's name. We saw it as a platform on which multiple people would build their solutions. And in the startup world, these types of things are called accelerators. So, our general thought was, "OK, we are going to accelerate innovation. Let's make the name Innovaccer." So that's how the name came to be. We didn't put too much thought into it, but it turned out to be fine.

We have always taken compliance and security as essential.

Regarding our compliance with HIPAA and HITRUST, we used third parties because we wanted the experts to help us get it right. Even today, I think a large part of R&D expenses goes toward compliance, data security, and things of that nature. The number of penetration tests that we run daily is scary at times, right? People are finding new ways to attack, new ways to do distributed denial of service attacks, and those sorts of things. I don't think a Chief Information Security Officer's job has ever been harder. We have always taken compliance and security as essential, like any other data and technology company right now. About 10% to 15% of our R&D expenses go to supporting security, which I think is generally much larger than other firms. People usually spend about 5%, but because we deal with healthcare data and information, we end up spending a lot more. We really didn't intend to spend more; it was just a function of doing the work that needed to be done and realizing it was about 15% a year. I'd like to spend less if there were an option to do so, but we have to do what we have to do.

Talent acquisition is a big place where our funders and advisors helped, especially the leadership team build out, not at the junior level but at the senior executive level and board creation. Jonathan Bush joined because he and the founder of WestBridge went to business school at Harvard together. And our CTO, Mike Sutten, came onboard because B Capital had worked with Kaiser in the past, and Mike was the CTO of Kaiser back then. I think those are the kinds of areas in which they have been very helpful. They also helped us understand that at this stage, you need this type of talent; at that stage, you should hire this type of talent. I mean, this is the first time we were doing this.

And while we have been a very first-principles company, the board and investors would offer help preemptively, which was very helpful. They helped us think about what we needed to do two or three years out so we could hire for the long term. I think a lot of founders make the mistake of hiring people when they need them, when really, you have to hire a person who will fit into that role two years from now. If they just fit the role today, then for a fast-growing company, you would grow out of them within two years. As a result, many startups keep changing their leadership teams quite often.

> ***I think it's important for every founder to have mentors like Sumir and Jonathan.***

Two of my primary mentors were Sumir Chadha, who was my first investor from WestBridge, and Jonathan Bush. I've been on the financial side of things because I'm not a technical founder. So, understanding the importance of money and things of that nature with Sumir and understanding healthcare, economics, and how things really work with Jonathan have been very helpful. I think it's important for every founder to have mentors like Sumir and Jonathan.

> ***You need to hire someone who is a little bit ahead of where you are.***

In addition to great mentors, we've had a stable, strong leadership team over the years. Dr. Nace has been here for six and a half years of the seven or eight years that we've been in healthcare. Mike has been with us for five years. We have a new CFO, who's been here for a year and a half, because as we were hitting scale, we needed a new CFO. But our last CFO was at the company for six years. So, I think hiring a little bit early, even when it feels like hiring a person of this stature is premature, gives you more right to expand into that size and scale you want to achieve – at least that is my sense. Because, like anyone coming in, they are just figuring out their way for the first six months. So, by the time they are ready to work in a fast-growth software company, the company has already grown 100%. You are now double the size during the six months the person was getting adjusted. Why did you even hire someone who may be a great fit for a $20 million company, but by the time they got ramped up, you were already at 50? You need to hire someone who is a little bit ahead of where you are.

> ***I think there is this broader sense of growth within the business that makes people feel accountable and have a sense of ownership across the board.***

And a lot of our growth is due to our stable team, I would say. Out of the first 100 people hired, 35 are still with the company ten years later. We hired a lot of them as 18- or 19-year-old kids, and now they are VPs within the company. I think there is this broader sense of growth within the business that makes people feel accountable and have a sense of ownership across the board. You're not stuck solving anyone else's problems. If they have a problem, they might come to me at some point, but I can be very assured that they have given it their best shot. I think that allows for unnatural scaling because with that level of trust, you can bend the laws of physics a little bit on how you grow.

I don't think that other healthcare software technology companies have grown at the pace that we have. A large part of the reason is that we have this incredibly committed team all around. I don't think initially they were the best in the world at anything because, at 19, it's hard to be the best in the world at anything. But over time, I think we all have learned a lot over the past ten years, really knowing everything inside and out from enterprise architectures to data models to marketing to go-to-market motions. We have an incredibly talented team at this point.

> ***At the $3B valuation, I think there was a little bit of a cultural shift that happened. I think employees started feeling a little bit more entitled.***

When we became a Unicorn, it was very relevant for us. We went to Napa and partied for two full days. I don't even remember those days. (We don't remember them because we drank too much, not because of anything else.) It was a big deal. It is a milestone that very few companies end up getting to, and we celebrated that quite a bit, but it didn't change anything in the company. At the $3 billion valuation, I think there was a little bit of a cultural shift that happened. I think employees started feeling a little bit more entitled. The employees seemed to think that anything they did would turn into gold and things like that. But the truth is that you must be on it all the time, right? If you let any of these [entitlement] ideas get into your head, then the downfall starts to happen. As that was starting to creep into our culture, I think downturn time started. We had layoffs, and I didn't even get a chance to correct it. The culture of entitlement seemed to self-correct with the layoffs.

> ***You're not working for a specific achievement because you're already proven. Instead, you can think about building something that is sustainable – how does it become a thing on its own.***

We really want to run this company for the long term. We're very motivated by the fact that we have a fantastic mission. There is so much to do. I would not want to do anything else; this is something that I really enjoy doing. If I got offered Satya [Nadella]'s job, maybe. But even then, I am so incredibly passionate about what we are trying to do and the problems we are trying to solve. I think all our founding team is like that, too – very committed to the mission. None of us really want to do anything else. So, there is longer-term thinking at this point when you hit these kinds of milestones. You're not working for a specific achievement because you're already proven. Instead, you can think about building something that is sustainable – how does it become a thing on its own. You begin to spend more time thinking about organizational structures, processes, frameworks, and things of that nature. When you are at the early stages, all these things are just boring. And who wants to do it, right? But now you start realizing that if you don't put processes in place to ensure the right outcomes, it's a problem. So, we're spending a lot more time figuring out what does a sustainable Innovaccer look like in ten years. We are still in our first decade, but what does the next decade look like? It's an important question in front of us now.

I think building and sustaining culture is the hardest.

I think building and sustaining culture is the hardest. You build it, and then it evolves without doing anything. I think the organization starts mirroring what the founders are doing. You can call culture anything, but I think if it is built on what the leadership team and founders are doing – that effectively becomes the culture, right? But to sustain a sense of that culture is very hard. When you reach 1,000 people, and hopefully at some time 5,000 or 10,000 people, you must ask: do the new recruits feel the same way or not? That is the real test of culture. A lot of my time goes into culture. We need to have the best-of-breed engineering culture, we need to party at times, and we need to be a happy place to work. I think that is very important for us, especially with my own clinical depression. We want to create a sense of happiness and purpose, which I think is very important from a cultural perspective. Not that I think we are perfect or anywhere near it, but I think the intent is very real from our standpoint.

The biggest thing I would say to other potential founders is that healthcare is not a get-rich-quick scheme.

The biggest thing I would say to other potential founders is that healthcare is not a get-rich-quick scheme. A lot of people jump into healthcare, seeing that $4 trillion TAM at the top, and that $4 trillion is being spent every year in this industry. They think, "We'll jump into it and make money one way or the other," and that is a very, very sure path to failure.

If you are going to build anything in healthcare, you need to be very long-term oriented, because anything of consequence in healthcare takes a lot of time, and adoption cycles are slow.

If you are going to build anything in healthcare, you need to be very long-term oriented, because anything of consequence in healthcare takes a lot of time, and adoption cycles are slow. People in healthcare are generally wary about new things, so if you're not up for the grind, this is not going to work out for you. If you want to build a healthcare technology company, know that you're committing at least a decade, if not more, before you will be anywhere near what people call successful.

7.5 Notes

Endnotes

1 https://innovaccer.com/
2 https://my.pitchbook.com/profile/85227-49/company/deals#deal-166841-83T
3 https://my.pitchbook.com/profile/85227-49/company/profile#deal-history

Chapter 8

Lunit

We were hoping to get customers, but we failed and got harsh feedback.

– Minhong Jang, Co-founder and CBO

8.1 Quick Facts

Website	https://www.lunit.io/en
Founded	2013
Mission	*Conquer cancer through AI*[1]
Founders	Donggeun Yoo, PhD https://www.linkedin.com/in/donggeun-yoo-90418598/ Kyunghyun Paeng https://www.linkedin.com/in/kyunghyun-paeng-b1163589/ Sunggyun Park https://www.linkedin.com/in/sunggyun-park-09ba61136/ Jungin Lee, PhD https://www.linkedin.com/in/jungin-lee-46220043/ Anthony Paek https://www.linkedin.com/in/anthony-paek/ Minhong Jang https://www.linkedin.com/in/minhong-jang-a031b229/

DOI: 10.4324/9781032711034-8

Unicorn status achieved	July 2022[2]
Funding rounds[3]	11 funding deals • April 2014–July 2022 • $0.10 million–$150 million
Notable funders	• HealthQuest Capital • SoftBank Ventures Asia • Guardant Health • Fujifilm

8.2 TLDR

Ideate

- Founded by six engineering students with diverse backgrounds in electrical engineering (EE), computer science, industrial engineering, and material science
- Initial idea focused on a fashion search engine using computer vision technology
- Pivoted to healthcare after feedback from investors and observing the subjective nature of medical image analysis
- Chose medical imaging due to its potential for global impact, collaboration with top-tier hospitals, and their ability to push the boundaries of accuracy through their technology, understanding that this enhanced precision is critical for better clinical outcomes

Build

- Developed an MVP for tuberculosis detection using deep learning technology
- Faced initial challenges in data collection and gaining acceptance from medical professionals
- Collaborated with the Korean National Tuberculosis Association and top Korean hospitals for data and validation
- Published research papers with renowned institutions like Seoul National University Hospital and UCSF to build credibility

Launch

- Launched a public demo website in 2016 to showcase AI capabilities and attract global interest

- Participated in the Radiological Society of North America (RSNA) event, leading to partnerships with global vendors like GE, Fujifilm, and Philips
- Secured Series A funding from Formation 8 and SoftBank Ventures Asia, which helped in further development and validation
- Achieved regulatory approval in Korea and began the process for FDA and CE mark approvals

Grow

- Expanded product offerings to include solutions for lung cancer, breast cancer, and tuberculosis
- Established partnerships with major medical device companies to distribute products globally
- Implemented a hybrid sales model, combining direct sales in Korea with global partnerships
- Received WHO recommendation for tuberculosis detection solution and expanded into 40 countries
- Achieved a market cap of $1.2 billion and continued to focus on improving accuracy and impact on patient outcomes

8.3 Meet the Founder

Minhong co-founded Lunit in 2013 to pioneer AI solutions for precision diagnostics and therapeutics, with a core focus on confronting cancer, one of the leading causes of death worldwide.

Minhong Jang

Lunit's advanced AI technology for medical imaging has earned significant international acclaim. Recognized by CB Insights as a leading company in both their "AI 100" and "Digital Health 150" lists, Lunit was also selected by the World Economic Forum as a "Technology Pioneer." Building on these achievements, Lunit was successfully listed on KOSDAQ (KOSDAQ: 328130) in July 2022.

Minhong led Lunit's radiology solution business, spearheading pivotal partnerships with global medical imaging technology leaders such as GE Healthcare, Philips, and Fujifilm. This strategic leadership drove the adoption of Lunit's solutions in hospitals across over 35 countries, enhancing day-to-day clinical workflows for better patient care. His innovative contributions were further recognized in 2021 when he was named to the prestigious MIT Technology Review "Korean Innovator Under 35" list.

Prior to Lunit, he gained valuable experience at InBody (KOSDAQ: 041830), a worldwide leader in body composition technology, where he devised online business strategies and analyzed customer behavior in the Home Health Department. Minhong holds a BS in Materials Science and Engineering and an MS in Management Engineering from KAIST.

8.4 Interview with Minhong Jang, Co-founder and CBO

When we started our company, we were just six engineering students. Anthony Paek was the one who gathered five other members, and we were all into the same music, like a club in undergrad school. We were into hip hop music, producing, rapping, and setting up stages, and Anthony was the sound engineer. So, we would all just hang out. I was a freshman, and he was four years older than me, but we just liked hanging out and sharing our music style. But he was a really great engineer. He initiated a study group with four of his friends. They studied computer vision because he was majoring in electrical engineering (EE), and other students were also EE or CS [computer science] or industrial engineering. Together, they worked to deepen their understanding of computer vision technology. They would conduct research papers, and after completing their research, they would go out and get a drink, like Korean alcohol, together.

> ***Maybe we can start a project together and maybe build a company.***

My undergraduate major was materials science. When I was in graduate school, I studied management engineering, essentially engineering with a management side to it. Anthony reached out to me and said that they were studying computer vision technology. I thought it was very interesting and said, "Maybe we can start a project together and maybe build a company." That turned into a project to make an interesting search engine. The idea was to take a photo of a fashion item with your cell phone, perform an Internet search of similar images from all the different websites, and then get a recommendation about similar available items. That was our idea, and though we struggled, we started that project at the university around 2013 and built an MVP.

We thought, maybe we can meet some nice investors, and we can be billionaires.

We built an MVP with the fashion item, and we went to Silicon Valley to meet investors because we watched the HBO drama "Startup."[4] We thought, maybe we can meet some nice investors, and we can be billionaires. That was the idea, and we met so many people because other Korean startups also got funding from US investors, like MEMEBOX. That company is a fashion, cosmetic, or commerce company based in Korea, but the CEO got funds from Pejman Nozad [of Pear VC], who was the first investor in Dropbox. In addition to investors, we also met with people who worked for eBay or Yahoo to showcase our solution, like a search engine. We were hoping to get customers, but we failed and got harsh feedback. "This is a very interesting project, but it is really difficult to change the fundamental method to search for clothes." And it was not really that accurate, either.

Maybe you guys can apply this technology to medical imaging.

So, we were disappointed, but we remembered that a random investor we met at the networking event happened to mention, "Maybe you guys can apply this technology to medical imaging." Anthony thought that it was an interesting idea. We met our friends who were pathologists, and they invited us to their lab. We observed how they read the pathology images, and it was highly subjective. We were shocked. Our friends just counted mitosis and assigned the grade, which was also very subjective. We asked our pathologist friends, "How old this method? How many years have pathologists been doing this job this way?" He said that this grade criterion was invented in 1960, so it's more than 50 years old. Again, we were really shocked at how subjective this was and had been.

We thought maybe AI or computer vision technology could change things and support doctors. But Anthony and I also started checking other industries, like advertising and security, because we were also contacted by Logitech, the webcam company. They wanted us to build a security engine for their home tenant, so that was also a very interesting topic. We checked all the possible ways to apply the technology, and we selected the medical application. We thought that pathology would be a very interesting area, and it could become a global company – a very big company. Also, Korean hospitals and Korean healthcare, in general, are great. So, if we collaborate with the top five university-level hospitals in Korea, maybe we could position ourselves at a global level. And that was how we changed our focus, using the same computer vision technology, from fashion to healthcare.

> ***Our first research topic was cervical cancer, a very big issue that already had some automation by that time from companies like Hologic.[5]***

Our first research topic was cervical cancer, a very big issue that already had some automation by that time from companies like Hologic.[5] But we recognized that it was particularly difficult to get the data. We were just very naive at the time.

Because we were building an image retrieval and computer vision technology company, we checked how many images are actually taken of which body part, using which modality. Chest images were the most common. When we researched the market, we realized there was already a computer-aided detection (CAD) solution in the United States for mammograms. So, we checked for clinical impact and learned that detecting lung cancer and breast cancer is very impactful and quite difficult to detect in 2D images. That was a very simple but powerful and logical flow.

> ***The perception from the medical community, from older, experienced doctors and professors, was that they thought medicine was an art.***

Initially, we visited some Korean hospitals to collect data through a research contract. But we faced significant difficulties in the beginning. The perception from the medical community, from older, experienced doctors and professors, was that they thought medicine was an art. They didn't think that software developers could provide a benefit to clinical professionals. They considered their work holistic, and they told us, "You are good engineers, but why are you doing this?" That was our first feedback from the university hospitals. So, this was in 2014, and we were struggling to collect the data. However, in 2015, DeepMind showcased AlphaGo in Korea. As a result, many doctors and intellectuals in Korea changed their perspective on AI. That event made it easier for us to collaborate with hospitals.

> ***[W]e thought that deep learning could beat any traditional machine learning and that was going to be our strength – we were going to apply it first.***

Our first MVP project was for tuberculosis detection. At that time, we didn't have many contacts within hospitals, but fortunately, we got a contact within the Korean National Tuberculosis Association. They had an ongoing project with another set of university engineers to develop a tuberculosis detection engine based on traditional machine learning technology. But we were already using deep learning in 2013, after the success of AlexNet in the ImageNet challenge.[6] On the basis of that event, we thought that deep learning could beat any traditional machine learning, and that was going to be our strength – we were going to apply it first. We applied deep learning technology to that project with a small amount of data from existing university researchers, and that was the "wow" moment. In two weeks, we had built the MVP; it was just a simple website. But the association was already doing a two-year project with another university, and we were all impressed at the results from this two-week MVP from Lunit. So, we started to dive deep with both projects, collect more data, and explore other areas like breast cancer.

Our academic backgrounds, which involved pursuing PhDs and master's degrees, meant we were accustomed to publishing papers on our findings. This was a significant factor in our decision to select the healthcare field. Unfortunately, our lack of direct experience in healthcare meant we were largely unfamiliar with the regulatory process. However, we recognized the critical importance of publications. Anthony and several other co-founders had already contributed to notable papers in other fields at an international level. Furthermore, we were aware that, as the six co-founders were not medical doctors, our capacity to delve beyond initial domain knowledge into deeper medical insights and truly understand customer perspectives, particularly those of doctors, was constrained. Consequently, we brought Brandon Suh on board as CMO. After successfully serving in the CMO role for two years, he transitioned to CEO, spearheading the company's global business expansion and actively leading global partnership strategies alongside me.

Going back to our MVP stage, we didn't know much about the healthcare industry, but we knew the importance of accuracy and writing publications. When we initiated our scalable research project with the Seoul National University Hospital, one of the most renowned hospitals in Korea, we were already thinking about how we needed to showcase our products' accuracy with publications co-authored with doctors. Doctors also wanted to publish with us, as they would become the first or second to participate in this kind of research project. So, there was this motivation on all sides, leading to a great win-win project for everyone.

To scale, however, we needed regulatory approval. Fortunately, on the mammography side, we could see the process that others had already gone through, and we read the documents that were submitted to the FDA, as well as the FDA guidelines that were frequently referred to. While we didn't understand the meaning of the statistics, the methodology, or the terminology, we could easily observe the information from the regulatory process of mammography.

> ***We went to the Korean FDA, and they invited Lunit to participate in a committee to develop the national AI and AI-based software as a medical device clinical study protocol and the regulatory guideline development.***

When we got the Series A round of funding, we also thought that our software could be recognized as a medical device. We went to the Korean FDA, and they invited Lunit to participate in a committee to develop the national AI and AI-based software as a medical device clinical study protocol, and the regulatory guideline development. I was part of that committee for about two years, and we built that guideline together with the government, hospitals, and industry people like me, plus other engineers, and professors.

For the traditional software, like the software used in mammography, the guidelines and how others conducted clinical studies are already there. But because deep learning is more like a "black box," we looked at the US FDA's guidelines specifically for AI clinical studies.[7] In Korea, the regulatory committee also followed other countries, reviewing their guidelines, especially the US guidelines. Korea not only tried to apply similar guidelines but also listened to comments from people in the industry and in government and came up with their own regulation for AI-based medical software.

We also had to conduct the clinical study based on that guideline, as our solution is considered a medical device. And because I was also building a solution that had patient risk, it was very clear to me that the guideline should be very logical with minimal burden. For example, what if the guideline recommended that every company do a prospective study? Well, that's nonsense. So, we made room in the guidelines to allow retrospective studies as well. I pursued the retrospective study strategy, and, in parallel, we communicated with the Korean FDA about our clinical trial protocol. We shared the published study we had already done on a small scale with the university hospital. It was all very logical, and we were able to accelerate our regulatory approval process because of the alignment between the guideline and our completed study.

When we started looking at global markets, we recognized how difficult it was to get regulatory approval, and we realized that it takes a very long time

When we started looking at global markets, we recognized how difficult it was to get regulatory approval, and we realized that it takes a very long time. As for the FDA, we contacted them and learned about the guidelines and pathways, including the pre-submission process. So, we prepared documentation before the submission and had a call with the FDA. We showed them our documentation and discussed the regulatory pathway. We asked, "How long does it take and what kind of clinical outcome we can pursue?" We not only got a clear understanding of the process but also realized that it would take a very long time.

For Europe, the CE mark is not that strict and a bit easier. For the United States, for example, we needed to test our solution with US citizens and diverse ethnic groups. We conducted a reader study.[8] We needed to both hire US doctors and do the study, so that's another reason why it took a long time. We learned a lot from the process with the Korean FDA, but we also learned more when we expanded to the United States and Europe.

Each solution, mammography and chest X-ray, had to go through the approval process – one by one – which took at least two years with the FDA.

Each solution, mammography and chest X-ray, had to go through the approval process – one by one – which took at least two years with the FDA. When we first started with the CE process a few years ago, we could leverage a Korean study or a reader study to get our CE mark, which took less than one year. But because of the changes to the EU's Medical Device Regulation (MDR),[9] compliance now takes more than two years there as well for each product. And now we have three solutions approved and deployed in more than 40 countries.

But this all started in Korea, which has a very unique healthcare system. It's a single-payer system from the government. When we initially started our company, we recognized that the Korean market is tiny, so we knew we would need to expand globally. Another reason is that in Korea, the average medical fee is not only quite cheap, but also Korean healthcare is very accessible. For example, we have about 60 million people in Korea, but about 45 million X-ray tests are conducted annually. I also regularly go to the hospital for annual checkups, and an X-ray test is the default level of care.

> ***We offered it for free as a research project, but we told the hospital that they would get the benefit of having a good reputation by using AI to double check the x-ray results. That was our initial offer, before we started selling the product.***

As a result, it was very easy to test if our MVP solution worked in the healthcare screening centers. At the time, we didn't have any business development team members at Lunit, so I went to the large healthcare checkup centers and offered to conduct the research project with them. We proposed analyzing all the X-rays from last year and this year to find anything suspicious, like a nodule or something. We offered it for free as a research project, but we told the hospital that they would get the benefit of having a good reputation by using AI to double-check the X-ray results. That was our initial offer, before we started selling the product. We were able to find suspicious cases that were initially read as normal when our solution was able to find a nodule on the image.

This was after our Series A, because before the funding round we didn't know much about the regulations. But once we had our MVP, we closed the Series A round from Formation 8, a VC based in the United States, which had invested in Oculus, which was eventually sold to Meta. As part of the due diligence process, we showcased our MVP, and then Formation 8 hired an external radiologist who checked our MVP. He believed that our solution was something new and that we could beat traditional CAD. So, that is how we got our Series A funding.

That kind of direct connection to the healthcare centers worked well for selling in Korea, but from a global perspective, as I mentioned, we recognized that the Korean market was tiny. We needed to go to other countries, but the FDA in the United States took a long time. We really didn't know what to do, as we were a bit naïve.

> ***They can co-sell our product, and we can be like NVIDIA or Intel, inside the larger solutions.***

We looked at the value chain, which includes the X-ray device, the AI, and the Picture Archiving and Communications System (PACS). We thought if we collaborated with the largest X-ray device vendors and the largest PACS vendors, they could reach out to all the global hospitals. They can co-sell our product, and we can be like NVIDIA or Intel, inside the larger solutions. That became our ideal scenario, so we started a global partnership strategy in 2015.

We didn't know anything about the Radiology Society of North America (RSNA), the largest conference and exhibition in the industry, hosted in Chicago every year. But the GE CMO invited us to that event, and that meeting initiated the conversation with the global vendors and was the start of our distribution channel. And by using this approach, we leveraged the systems integrations that had already been done by the global vendors; we didn't have to build it ourselves. But it wasn't quick! We met GE in 2015, and the contract was signed in 2020. It took five years because of their internal organizational changes and project priorities. We met Fujifilm in 2016 and got the contract signed in 2018. We met Phillips in 2017 and signed the contract in 2020. So, it took about three years to get these contacts because we were just a small startup, and they were global companies worth millions or billions of dollars.

We learned that credibility was and is super important.

We learned that credibility was and is super important. While we truly believed in our solution, gaining credibility from users and doctors – gaining that trust – only came through publishing many, many papers with the Korean University and other universities in the United States. The first one was UCSF [University of California at San Francisco], and we also published some papers with MGH [Massachusetts General Hospital].

Those papers documenting the science behind Lunit were very fruitful and made a strong case for our technology. Customers always compared the various AI vendors, and they often had their own team developing their own AI solution. So, it was always a comparison between Lunit and other solutions. We were always confident in our accuracy. When we first initiated the collaboration with Fujifilm, it became very successful in Japan and was the first AI project with an X-ray device. Then, GE and Philips recognized that Lunit was working well with Fujifilm. Using our NVIDIA/Intel inside strategy, we decided to work with everyone, and that is how we initiated that strategy.

But what does a global launch mean as a small startup?

Our initial feedback from hospitals was positive, primarily because they thought they could find more cases of lung cancer or other suspicious cases. So, we thought we had enough positive results to go global. But what does a global launch mean as a small startup?

> ***What's even more interesting is that Fujifilm checked our website, and they had already tested our demo with their data set. And that is how we started the engagement with them as a global vendor.***

We decided that, in addition to working with the device vendors, we should gather quotes from every university and every hospital we are working with and use them on our website. In addition, on our website, we built the capability for anyone to upload an X-ray image and see the AI-generated results. We had to be very careful about this and strongly disclose that this demo was not for clinical use. We quickly checked with the US attorney about doing this, and we learned that it was possible if we used the disclaimer that it was not for clinical use. So, we launched the website with that capability in 2016, and at the RSNA event, one year later, we realized that RSNA is the biggest exhibition in the radiology field. We also decided to have a small booth and present one clinical paper at the event. It was all budgeted and timed to promote the website on news wires at the same time the conference was happening. It was quite amazing because there were many radiologists from different countries very interested in this project. What's even more interesting is that Fujifilm checked our website, and they had already tested our demo with their data set. And that is how we started the engagement with them as a global vendor. It was not only a creative strategy but also quite a risky initiative. We eventually closed the demo site because of the potential risk and medical laws.

Some of the risky issues with that demo site included privacy and security. When we launched that website, we deleted all the images after the analysis. And before a user uploaded the images with the personal information, we anonymized all the personal information. All of this was clearly stated on the website and was approved by our US lawyers. We also got consent from the users before they used the demo site. It's important to say that when you deal with large, global companies, they have tons of different compliance rules that you must follow. It can be very burdensome to a small startup, but it's also an important issue. And because we were using personal healthcare data, data security was something we had to handle as well.

But when we were working with hospitals, they had already collected the data. We just analyzed it, and we shared the statistics. That is how we worked on the first paper with UCSF. One of our founders flew to UCSF and stayed a week to analyze it together with his UCSF counterparts. Everything at that point was done on-prem to reduce risks.

Our expansion strategy was very much a hybrid model.

When we initiated our global strategy, we developed a clustering approach. While it was nice to think that the global device partners would sell our products, we learned that each market has different players and approaches. We realized that we also needed to focus on customers and the market, like we had in Korea, where we are not working with any global vendors. In Korea, we were distributing our product mainly by ourselves. We also recruited local employees to generate leads, like a direct sales channel. They also had a second role, which was to collaborate with the global vendors to promote our solution and educate them on it. Our expansion strategy was very much a hybrid model.

And we also looked at our go-to-market approach in stages. First, we targeted device manufacturers; hospitals were second; and government or payers like insurance companies were third. Our sales ended up with about 50%–60% coming from device vendors and about 30% coming from hospitals because we could increase their return on investment (ROI), maybe increasing their productivity and decreasing the number of cases they were losing to competitors. In Australia, the government tried to embrace our AI technology for their breast cancer screening system to replace one doctor with AI because they have a two-doctor, double-reading system. And so, Lunit was selected to take the place of one of those readings. In areas where the government is the payer, like Korea, Japan, and Australia, our solution is integrated into the reimbursement process. But the bottom line is that we lead with the ROI scenario for marketing, especially with hospitals.

We knew we were on the right track when we started getting great feedback from patients and doctors.

We knew we were on the right track when we started getting great feedback from patients and doctors. One time, a patient came into the ER due to a skiing accident, and the doctors wanted to immediately perform the traditional surgery. Fortunately, that hospital had the Lunit solution, and Lunit can detect suspicious lung nodules. In this case, the patient was diagnosed with lung cancer because of our technology. We thought, "Wow, we're really making an impact on society!" Our solution also supports tuberculosis in developing countries and was recommended by the WHO as well. So, with that kind of impact, like replacing one doctor in a double-reading scenario in Sweden or Australia, there is less of a wait for image readings for breast cancer, for example. When we saw the impact, we *felt* it, and it was a very proud moment for us. It's the impact on people's lives that motivates us.

> ***For us, it's more important to use our technology to detect more cancers, at an early stage, to save more lives.***

Lunit is still not a profitable company. The market cap is about $1.2 billion, making us a Unicorn, but it doesn't have much significance. It carries symbolic value and serves as a title, reflecting a certain achievement, but that's about all. For us, it's more important to use our technology to detect more cancers at an early stage to save more lives

To other digital health founders, I would tell them it takes longer than expected. I recently was reading a story in a peer-reviewed journal that stated it takes 17 years for any new technology to be introduced and reach the mass market in a medical setting. I didn't know that. For other founders, you need to know that, first, the digital healthcare field is really designed to be a marathon, not a sprint. And second, healthcare systems differ significantly from country to country. Nevertheless, if [you begin with] a healthcare market that is small with a single-payer system like Korea, as Lunit did, you must aim globally from the start. It might be different for a startup in the United States or China, as they might be able to be Unicorns in their home markets. But this is not the case for other, smaller countries.

> ***I think the team's vision and the mission should be very clear because, as I mentioned, it's really a long journey and it is very complicated.***

Lastly, I think the team's vision and the mission should be very clear because, as I mentioned, it's really a long journey, and it is very complicated. To attract great people, the company must have a clear vision and a clear mission. Otherwise, all the talented people would just go to Microsoft or one of the other tech companies.

Right before we started planning the IPO, the leadership team reshaped our vision to read, "Conquer Cancer through AI." This is our vision now and our mantra both inside and outside the company. I think that resonates with everyone.

8.5 Notes

Endnotes

1 https://www.lunit.io/en/company
2 https://my.pitchbook.com/profile/90200-08/company/deals#deal-200170-81T
3 https://my.pitchbook.com/profile/57380-68/company/profile#insights
4 StartUp (TV Series 2016–2018) – IMDb.
5 https://www.hologic.com/
6 https://image-net.org/challenges/LSVRC/2012/
7 More on FDA guidelines for Software as a Medical Device https://www.fda.gov/medical-devices/digital-health-center-excellence/software-medical-device-samd
8 More on reader studies https://pubmed.ncbi.nlm.nih.gov/29653758/
9 More on MDR https://www.medical-device-regulation.eu/2019/07/11/mdr-article-61-clinical-evaluation/

Chapter 9

Omada Health

We didn't launch until we were on V3 of our product.

– Sean Duffy, Co-founder, CEO

9.1 Quick Facts

Website	https://www.omadahealth.com/
Founded	2011
Mission	*Our virtual-first, integrated care programs help people make lasting health changes that truly change their lives. That's why organizations choose our data-driven care solutions to drive lower costs and better outcomes.*[1]
Founders	Sean Duffy https://www.linkedin.com/in/seanpduffy/ Adrian James https://www.linkedin.com/in/adrianbjames/
Unicorn status achieved	Feb 2022[2]
Funding rounds[3]	Seven funding deals • May 2011–June 2023 • Range from $0.02 million in seed to $193 million E round • IPO May 2025

DOI: 10.4324/9781032711034-9

Leading funders from Series E round[4]	• Fidelity Management & Research Company (lead) • aMoon • Perceptive Advisors • Wellington Management • Civilization Ventures

9.2 TLDR

Ideate

- Concept originated during Sean Duffy's time in medical school, inspired by his background in neuroscience and interest in technology
- Co-founded with Adrian James at IDEO, focusing on digital health opportunities
- Identified a gap in healthcare for prediabetes and metabolic diseases, emphasizing the need for persistent support between visits
- Aimed to create a proactive and longitudinal approach to healthcare, reducing the feeling of isolation among patients

Build

- Developed initial prototypes using off-the-shelf tools and visual design mockups
- Secured a technical co-founder and raised a seed round to expand the team
- Conducted early trials and gathered data to validate the concept
- Focused on creating a seamless user experience with cellular-connected scales and a supportive care team

Launch

- Launched the company by spinning out from IDEO and securing initial Angel investment
- Participated in Rock Health's accelerator program, gaining early support and resources
- Engaged early customers through pilots and built trust by delivering on promises

Grow

- Expanded product offerings from prediabetes to include diabetes, hypertension, and musculoskeletal care

- Achieved significant milestones, including enrolling over one million members
- Secured partnerships with major organizations like Costco and expanded nationally
- Focused on maintaining high standards of customer deployment and support
- Continued to innovate and expand product offerings, aiming for long-term impact on healthcare

9.3 Meet the Founder

Sean Duffy

Sean Duffy is the Co-founder and CEO of Omada Health, a between-visit care provider for prediabetes/obesity, diabetes, hypertension, and musculoskeletal disorders. He has dedicated his professional life to harnessing the cross-functional impact of technology, design, and care delivery to transform care experiences for patients. As a former MD/MBA candidate at Harvard, he also holds a BS in neuroscience from Columbia University. He has written extensively about digital health and the future of healthcare in *The New England Journal of Medicine*, *The Wall Street Journal*, *Forbes*, and *TechCrunch*, among other publications. Before Omada, Sean worked at both Google and IDEO.

9.4 Interview with Sean Duffy, CEO and Co-founder

In medical school, I studied neuroscience in undergrad at Columbia, and I'd always been somewhat of a computer geek growing up. What drew me to healthcare was that it felt like a good place to have a career and give back. But at night, when I graduated in 2006 from undergrad, I was not cracking open my biochemistry textbook. I was reading tech blogs and looking at the latest in Silicon Valley. I got cold feet about going straight to medical school, even though I had done my premed requirements.

I ended up finding a job at Google and worked there for a couple of years. I began to realize that the world wasn't so black and white, and I went to medical school, enrolling in Harvard's MD MBA program. As you progress through the program, the school guides you to take an internship that blends business and medicine, and they usually set you up with a job at Mass General or Brigham, or some other local health system.

But I knew some of the folks at IDEO, the design firm in the valley, and I asked if I could spend an internship there. They said yes, so I went to IDEO and ended up working really closely with Adrian James, who's my cofounder from IDEO. He and I were given a budget to look at opportunities in digital health and the state of the landscape at that moment in time.

I noticed that my friends from Google were very enthusiastic about wearables, Fitbits, and steps trackers. And then my medical school classmates were asking, "What is the clinical evidence behind these tools and what disease areas are the companies targeting?"

We asked ourselves how one might build a more evidence-based digital health company, and then, subsequent to that, what are the care areas that really matter most for digital? That led us to a recognition about care between doctor's visit experiences, because in certain care areas, patients need this persistence of support. That led us to start the business with metabolic disease, prediabetes, and weight, just given the crisis in these disease areas and the realization that support is needed.

> ***We sat in people's homes in a couple of areas across the country, who had prediabetes and just asked what the healthcare world had offered them.***

We decided to use some time and energy to explore the concept, and then we became really inspired. We sat in people's homes in a couple of areas across the country who had prediabetes and just asked what the healthcare world had offered them. The answer was basically nothing. We quickly recognized that patients were falling into cracks.

We ended up deciding, yes, this was what we're going to do, and we spun the company out of IDEO.

Then I went back to my dean and asked for a year off from medical school. I never went back.

We came up with the name Omada because it means group or team in Greek, and we wanted [the process of getting healthcare] not to feel lonely. For example, if you have diabetes, you can feel like you're an island by yourself. We had this concept that a community of peers, clinicians, and meaningful social relationships would really matter. Additionally, building a company is a team sport, so we liked that aspect of the name as well. We also frankly couldn't come up with any better options, so that led to Omada.

We started with some visual design mockups and prototypes, using off-the-shelf tools. Once we had a general sense of the task at hand, we recognized we needed to find a technical cofounder, so I called up Andrew DiMichele, my friend from Colombia and an incredible engineer. He was willing to join as a technical cofounder.

We dove into the deep end and burned through our bank accounts a little bit until we were able to raise capital. Then the three of us really got started, and we went out to raise a seed round. We were able to secure a little bit of Angel investment and hung tight, keeping the headcount to just the three of us for a bit. Once we raised a little bit more, we modestly expanded the team.

> ***[W]e worked quickly to get prototypes in front of users. We used it to learn, and that learning fed into the next cycle of development, keeping up our momentum.***

Then, to get to the core of the idea and business model, we worked quickly to get prototypes in front of users. We used it to learn, and that learning fed into the next cycle of development, keeping up our momentum. The old world of taking three years to build something and then launching it doesn't tend to be as successful. It's important to build quickly, get reactions and feedback, and then get the next revision. We even did a prototype where we just used an off-the-shelf community tool to get a group of patients together, and I acted as their health coach. We essentially ran an intervention with nothing. While that seemed like a throwaway prototype, we did have more technical components connected, so we could scale and expand from there.

We went through three more of those cycles before we started to lay the real technical foundations of what we have today. We only started having conversations with clinicians and prospective customers when we had the third version of the prototype. At that time, we had 102 people that we were supporting on the platform, so it was a bit more real.

But I was green to enterprise healthcare. I had worked at Google as an individual contributor and then went to medical school for a year. So, I could read clinical trial documents, and I had empathy for the medical profession. But I didn't know anything about the business of the US healthcare system. It was basically me just trying to talk to every smart person I could and, more or less, praying that I'd get lucky. At the end of the day, you need to be willing to learn and listen and seek mentorship from people who've been on the block. I found myself going to just about any conference, talking to anyone who would pay attention, which was really hard, especially if your connections in the industry are limited. Fortunately, it started to work.

I think our first customers mostly came from introductions from either medical directors or people inside a plan, an employer, or a health system. These were people who had a bone to pick with this tsunami of disease that we're facing and continue to face as a country. So, they just made a bet to work with us, and they liked the preliminary data from that prototype.

I remember a meeting with the medical director of a health plan we wanted to work with. We sat down, and the director said they were considering us for a contract. He said,

> *Sean, look at us. Look at the conference room. I see your whole company. I'm thinking of writing a 5-year contract with you to support our most important client. What confidence do I have that you are going to be here in 5 years?*

It was a pivotal moment. I said we were backed by great investors that are committed to a long-term mission. But what I really wanted to say is, "If you sign this contract, we'll be just fine."

> ***[E]nterprise healthcare is very risk averse, and you need to approach the market knowing you need to earn trust.***

For startup founders, it's always the chicken and egg, needing customers to get more customers. Then you get to the final details, and they ask, "Show us your implementation plan. What other customers do you have?" And we're like, what plan? Our goal was to learn alongside our customers. In the early days, passion could get the job done. However, enterprise healthcare is very risk-averse, and you need to approach the market knowing you need to earn trust.

One of the things we did from the time we were established as three people was to call ourselves a *digital health* company. We never used the word startup because we recognized that these organizations are taking on substantial risk working with a young company. Not only do you have to convince them of your value proposition, but also you have to convince them that you're worth the investment, even while the company is at a very early age.

This is a little bit of an oversimplification, but you have four tracks to scale:

1. Product
2. Go-to-market
3. Clinical validation
4. Company DNA

You want to progress in all four, working to further each according to that month's or that quarter's needs. But all of that depends on having a product.

To reiterate, we really started talking to clients or potential clients when we had version 3, which was something that worked and they could use. It was important that they tell us, "Hey, we love this." Then they could actually buy, and we felt like we could deploy successfully.

I don't know whether there's a generic rubric for an early-stage company, because one big customer could pull you in one direction, and that means you have to pull forward more quickly in some areas or hold back in others, while trying to find capital to build a team.

> ***Forget about building the team and focus on what work needs to be done for the next chapter of the company. And then once you're crisp on that, the people, resources, or anything else you need is kind of a byproduct, a secondary consideration.***

I think the mistake that I sometimes see early companies make is raising funds and then hiring a team. It's important to be really very, very clear about what, specifically, is the work that needs to be done. Forget about building the team and focus on what work needs to be done for the next chapter of the company. And then once you're crisp on that, the people, resources, or anything else you need is kind of a by-product, a secondary consideration.

Our value proposition was always clear from the start. There was some refinement on how we told the story, but the value proposition was always clear. If you start with the chronic disease, the epidemiology, and the associated cost, it's pretty intuitive to folks who live in this space: the way that this country currently supports diabetes, for example, is massively inadequate. It was also clear that we hit the mark with our early prototypes, confirming that you couldn't just build a tech-only solution, nor a people-only solution. We also realized that we needed hardware, and we needed to own that experience and get the data back for analysis. We needed to own the full experience.

What took us time was figuring out how to sell within the enterprise healthcare landscape. There were plenty of learnings from successes and mistakes in the early days. The early successes were attributable to customers who really believed in our mission and the problem we were trying to solve.

Their team sat me down and said, "Sean, are we going to break you? We break vendors all the time." But I replied, "I give you my commitment we will work the problem."

One company that's been part of our journey for a long time is Costco. They began in a couple of states, and then they liked what they experienced. We didn't disappoint them. In fact, we exceeded their expectations, and they were ready to scale us nationally. Their team sat me down and said, "Sean, are we going to break you? We break vendors all the time." But I replied, "I give you my commitment we will work the problem." We recognized that (back to my comments on trust), if you fall short on excellence post-contracting, you are creating a massive headwind because it spreads in the market, and you become known as not being able to deliver on your commitment. So, we put a lot of energy into making sure that our customer deployments went well, and that continues to be our approach to this day. I mean, that is job number one. We give it our all to make sure that everything goes excellently for our customers.

[I]t was clear that she really cared in a different way and wanted to make an impact – all the characteristics of an early adopter.

When we landed at Costco in our third year, I don't even think we had a sales team. I was doing all of the sales. I didn't know anything about sales, but I could communicate effectively, so when I reconnected with the benefits leader, it was clear that she really cared in a different way and wanted to make an impact – all the characteristics of an early adopter. As an entrepreneur, the quicker you can bucket potential partners to pursue now versus later, the better off the company will be.

[As for accelerators], we had just left IDEO and were launching the company, and I got wind that Halle Tecco was building something called Rock Health. I met her, and she was like, "Oh, I'm working on this healthcare accelerator," as she called it back then. They didn't take equity, but they offered grants as a non-profit organization. She asked me if I wanted to apply, and I'm thinking – sure, free money, free office space, and a community. Sign me up! Halle was cool, and we were in their first cohort, even painting and helping them set up their first office. So, we end up being part of the first cohort at Rock Health, and they have become a key part of the digital health ecosystem to this day.

Rock Health launched much in the same way as we did. They, too, had to earn the right to be at the party. There were lots of critics talking about tech-forward people not knowing anything about healthcare, and they said that about me, too. But fast forward to today, and here we all are.

Today, we are a provider and must follow all the regulations of any other provider. We have to abide by the same sort of federal and state data and privacy protection laws that any other provider would. HIPAA is table stakes. But given where we sit, we have to pay attention to all the agencies. For example, all the hardware we use is FDA-regulated. Our partners and suppliers manage all of that, but we fit right into the provider landscape.

I remember in the early Omada days, the regulatory environment was far more ambiguous, so we probably spent about $50,000 to $100,000 on FDA consultants, and they all told us different things because this space was so new. But the regulations have really evolved and matured, which improves things across the ecosystem.

> ***We started thinking in terms of creating compassionate intelligence, and what we would need to build to support that.***

From a technology standpoint, we started with the core concepts and the recognition from the early days that to do the job right, we had to create kind of sense of empathy. So, our approach was much more about connecting people with amazing technology and design experiences. We started thinking in terms of creating compassionate intelligence and what we would need to build to support that. That led to thinking about the life cycle of a member, where someone signs up, then they get the needed hardware to handle their condition, in this case, pre-diabetes, to start. We would just mail them a cellular-connected scale that worked out of the box, but it also had to pass what I call "the mom test." My mom is not going to pair a Wi-Fi scale with her home network. Frankly, she'd be calling me to do that. So, we had to make sure it worked out of the box.

Once the scale is connected, the push notification comes in saying the scale is connected, and then you meet your care team, your health coach, and other members with your condition. Everyone gets to know the patient as a person, and then you can structure that with a product experience and achieve your goals. Additionally, there's this whole infrastructure of content, with social layers inside the program. The solution enables goal tracking and goal setting, using the infrastructure that helps support the patient while aligning the patient with their care team on what the next month looks like, essentially helping the patient stay on target not just this month, but for the next three months, iterating along the way.

We often joke that there are ten digital health businesses inside Omada because there are so many parts to the solution. You can find fitness trackers, or you can find great health education content or social healthcare or a whole host of other services. But we also recognize that patients need all the pieces.

But as far as our infrastructure goes, we are built on AWS, even though I came from Google. I think at that point in time, the Google Enterprise Cloud was pretty early and immature, and users had to have their code in Python, if my memory serves me. I don't think that's the case now, but we had selected from the Ruby on Rails stack.

There's an interesting story about this. We thought we were going to have to host everything on-prem. At that time, AWS wouldn't do anything in compliance with HIPAA, and they wouldn't sign Business Associate Agreements. What ended up happening was that there was a refresh of HIPAA that passed, and there was the secondary implication that nobody saw coming. In the previous regulations, it said that if you had patient health information (PHI) on your databases and you didn't want it there or didn't ask for someone to put it there, you got a pass. However, in this refresh, it said that if you had PHI, you had to delete it. If you're Amazon, you can't just go deleting people's data. Literally overnight, all the companies like Amazon and Google had to find a way to become HIPAA compliant. We popped bottles of champagne because this was going to fundamentally change things for us in a positive way.

Our first board members came with our Series A and subsequent rounds mostly included lead investors taking a board seat. And when it comes down to it, it's the person that joins that matters most.

As for our investors, in the seed stage of Omada, we never picked up any board members because they wrote mostly smaller checks. Our first board members came with our Series A, and subsequent rounds mostly included lead investors taking a board seat. And when it comes down to it, it's the person who joins that matters most. In the early funding rounds, the focus is on strategic alignment and the vision for the business. If you don't have that alignment, it can cause real problems. Omada Health is very blessed in that we've had a great board. Starting from the early days, our board members were aligned with where we wanted to take the business. They were aligned with us wanting to be an enterprise and be a provider, and they were willing to suffer through the complexity of operating with the existing healthcare system. And that has been a real blessing.

I think the best board members tend to ask the most questions. Even if the board members feel they may know the answer, their questions are a method to prompt management to think about a certain issue.

As I reflect now on the Omada board, I realize that being an excellent board member is a craft – a real skill. There are plenty of unexcellent board members, and there are plenty of excellent board members. There are jobs they should do and jobs they shouldn't. Sometimes I get asked, "Did your board members help you close customers?" And the answer is no. Your board members should help you evaluate your organization and ask hard questions, like, "Do you have the organizational capability to close customers?" I think the best board members tend to ask the most questions. Even if the board members feel they may know the answer, their questions are a method to prompt management to think about a certain issue.

But it's also important to build a relationship with the board that invites vigorous debate towards the right end for the business and shareholders, seeking truths and not being afraid to debate in a productive way.

As a founder, you are always dealing with an infinite to-do list. A good board kind of pulls you up, forces you to look around a little bit, and then drops you back down into the day-to-day operations. They might draw your attention to a trend in the market, or the financial realities of your business, or the unit economics. Having their assistance to pull you up and reflect is a very helpful function for the board. Having a board to support the management and really listening to the founders is helpful. But it's also important to build a relationship with the board that invites vigorous debate toward the right end for the business and shareholders, seeking truths and not being afraid to debate in a productive way. I think there are boards and board members that are just good at that – building constructive tension.

Maybe they can help with executive connections, etc. But they are not your sales team. We feel very lucky with the board that we have. They're very engaged, and it really does matter, especially in the early days.

Launching is rarely the big bang that people often think about. From my perspective, it's the exception rather than the rule. It's more like a lot of little pops. It's funny that sometimes you'll hear even today, "Oh my gosh, the digital landscape is so noisy. Who knows which way it's going to go?" And I remember thinking, we are 11 people! How are we going to punch through the noise?

To rise above the noise, you need persistence and clarity of message. If you can't be succinct with what you are, you'll get caught in the quagmire.

To rise above the noise, you need persistence and clarity of message. If you can't be succinct with what you are, you'll get caught in the quagmire. As a team and as a company, we have made sure that our dual mission shines through in that we want to build.

We wanted to build an enormously successful business that's hugely financially successful, and we thought that the best route to achieve that goal was to fix the health access and quality issue across the country.

I do think that companies with clear, articulated missions have a better chance of breaking through from a shared voice standpoint. And it's the daily focus on the mission that gets the job done versus just hanging tight in the closet, and in two weeks, launching and praying we get some media coverage. Even if that does happen, you get a pop, and then that dies away anyway.

When we look at the business, there are a couple of "eras" for the business, and there is a job to be done in each era. Era One was more focused on, "Will the solution work?" In the early days, we started working on multiple prototypes, focused on getting our data in publications, and running trials. We recognized that even if I were to go back to my medical school classmates with our solution, they're not going to say, "Sure, we trust you, Sean!"

So, once we knew it worked, then it was all about, will anyone buy it? We asked ourselves, "How do we implement it successfully with our first customers and iron out the playbook?" Era Two became ensuring that anybody could buy it and we could deploy it. Era Three was, "Can we scale repeatedly?" We were focused on delivering on our promises and not disappointing customers. Then we built the organization as we began to scale customers and deliver effectively. Era Four was about determining if our customers would buy more from us. So, we expanded from prediabetes to diabetes, hypertension, and musculoskeletal care. Then we thought, ok, let's swing big and see what level of scale we can hit. This involved a lot of company building and maturation related to operations. Last year, we crossed the cumulative 1,000,000 enrollment mark, and it's like it really does take a machine to scale. Using a factory analogy, it's pretty easy to help one person or build one prototype car, but it's really hard to manufacture cars to scale, and we needed to think in a similar way.

When you expand and become multi-product, it may never feel like the perfect time because it's hard to do.

When you expand and become multi-product, it may never feel like the perfect time because it's hard to do. However, building additional products is great for the business and serves your customers better. We had the voice of the customer asking, "My gosh, Omada, could you do this? Could you do that?" And from a clinical perspective, it was within our thesis on the company's work. But I think we thought it was going to be much easier than it actually was, which is something you'll hear pretty consistently from CEOs and founders who've gone from single to multi-product.

There are two things working against you. First, you've spent the entire history of the business talking about that one solution – that one thing. So, it took a while for the world to view Omada as broader than just prediabetes and weight. Even years later, we still hear, "Oh, you do diabetes, now?" It takes a bit of time for the new reality to catch on. Then, from a sales motion standpoint, there's a lot of new infrastructure. Some of it is small and tactical, like the fact that we had literally created our CRM for one product, including all the tagging and the data infrastructure. And now, we are thinking, well, shoot. Now I have this deal and that deal, this one in the pipeline for that product, but not this one. There is a huge operational piece, and before you know it, things get very, very complex. Then there's a sales training piece, where all of a sudden, we realized it's probably too much to ask for one sales rep to be an expert in four clinical areas.

You need to ask yourself some really difficult questions. How do we staff for the product? Support it? Facilitate a successful go-to-market in an area where you're doing a lot of different things?

Once you get it done, you have a repeatable infrastructure. But expanding is a massive build and a huge commitment, for sure.

Healthcare is really siloed, which is why we felt what we were doing from a care model standpoint was so important. Today's healthcare experience for someone right now is you meet my primary care doc to talk about your diabetes for 15 minutes. They ask you to come back in six months, and you have nothing to fill in the gaps and no social support. No infrastructure, no people, no community, nothing. It is our obligation to fix that.

If I ever founded something new, there are many mistakes I wouldn't make, but most of those are product or even go-to-market types of things. It's more about building anything for the first time. When we started Omada, I had never hired anybody. I didn't know how to run a team, or what a VP of sales was, or a VP of finance, or a VP of operations. I'd read a book called *The 10-Day MBA* and another book called *The Entrepreneurial Guide to Business Law,* and all of Paul Graham's posts, and then started running.

> ***The two go-to-market lessons I tend to put forward for entrepreneurs are to first, really understand the sales cycles of your buyers.***

The two go-to-market lessons I tend to put forward for entrepreneurs are, first, to really understand the sales cycles of your buyers. I didn't have a good handle on that for the first couple of years. You need to try and live in their shoes. When do they make decisions? How do they evaluate partners? What happens in January versus August versus September versus October with your customer? When is their budgeting cycle? Until you can map that, you can't figure out how to manage the business. Let's say you launch something in September; no one cares until the next selling or budgeting cycle.

> ***Second, you need to put a lot of thought into pricing and packaging and make it as simple as possible to buy.***

Second, you need to put a lot of thought into pricing and packaging, and make it as simple as possible to buy. Founders also need to recognize that they are working with a procurement team, and their job is to take 10% off or get the best deal possible. In fact, the procurement team is probably bonused on that.

I know we didn't put as much thought into the pricing or the packaging.

> ***From a first principle standpoint, I think pricing should be tied to the value you're delivering, which means just charging for those people who sign up.***

There are a couple of pricing models that are common in our space. Previously, companies would price based on per employee or per member/per month, known as PEM or PMPM. So, if you have 100,000 lives at an employer and you charge a dollar for everybody, regardless of whether they use it. While I didn't know anything about the history of pricing in healthcare, that model never made sense to me. From a first-principle standpoint, I think pricing should be tied to the value you're delivering, which means just charging those people who sign up.

Perhaps we were naïve to never have a [per member per month] PMPM model, choosing to charge only when someone signed up. Frankly, that is how the world works in other industries, and our clients liked our approach because it was counter to what they were hearing from others. Plus, our customers thought it was lower risk because if nobody used it, they didn't have to pay.

The by-product of this approach was that it made us focus. We had to make sure we were really good at getting people in the door. We also had to make sure we were delivering on the value for the member. I think you'll find the occasional benefits consultant out there who will say, "Omada killed the PMPM model." Interestingly, a lot of people said to me in the early days, "You cannot build a business without a PMPM. It just won't be possible. You'll get just too much irregularity in the volume, and you won't be able to predict it." But we liked the approach. It's simple. Full stop. There's no some weird, crazy charge for this or a fee for that.

So, it was special last year when we crossed a million. That was a really great feeling – it's probably the thing I'm most proud of to date.

One of the big milestones was crossing the million-enrollment mark. That was pretty special. Have we made a difference in the epidemiology of the country? No, clearly the job is bigger than what we've done. But it took so much energy to get 3,000 people to sign up. The number of walls we had to bust through was pronounced just to get to 3,000 members. So, it was special last year when we crossed a million. That was a really great feeling – it's probably the thing I'm most proud of to date.

It's not good to chase a valuation as an entrepreneur. You should chase after solving a customer's problem.

When we reached Unicorn status, we really didn't consider it much. In fact, if anything, we tried to downplay it internally. It's not good to chase a valuation as an entrepreneur. You should chase after solving a customer's problem. You do find entrepreneurs who will say, "I cannot wait to get that billion-dollar valuation." Maybe they're signing up for terms they shouldn't to support becoming a Unicorn or working with folks that don't understand their business well enough. It's not good to chase a valuation as an entrepreneur. You should chase solving a customer's problem.

For some people at the company, becoming a Unicorn may have been meaningful, but for me, it didn't feel like much. Even when we were doing the funding round, I was thinking to myself as I looked at the term sheet, "Well, this is interesting. Based on the term sheet they provided, I think that would make us valued over a billion after this financing." I almost didn't know it. And it wasn't that meaningful for me because I don't think it really means anything. I don't think the orientation should focus on valuation.

We say this very vocally, internally, "Look, you should be a little bit embarrassed of your last year's self."

One other thing that's always been helpful to me is to imagine what the company's going to be doing or need to have as a leader, not ten years out and not even three years out. But literally, what the company needs to be doing next year. Every year, I've asked myself, "What does tomorrow's CEO of Omada need to do and be?" And I try to extract myself from that line of thinking so I can be more objective. Then I make sure I have mentors who have lived the experience to guide me to that next milestone. I need to make sure I have the self-awareness to know that I may not have some of the skills. My focus becomes figuring out and piecing together what the next version of Sean needs to be. We say this very vocally, internally: "Look, you should be a little bit embarrassed of your last year's self." That should be the goal. Because the business changes so fast and the needs of the business change so fast, the only way to keep up is to find the things you need to be doing a year ahead and find the people with the skills to get you there. The advisors and friends who I've learned the most from have helped me stay a little bit in front of our needs – but not too far in front – and we just keep inching farther and farther ahead.

For example, we're proud of the 1,000,000 members, but over the next decade, I want to make sure that 1 million turns into 10 million and beyond. Therefore, we're all oriented toward leveraging the assets we have, which is a strong customer base with good momentum in the market. This is a chance to properly swing and create the orientation that we're still at the starting line, finally able to actually do what we've wanted to do. Which is exciting.

Resources

The Book That Helped the Co-Founder and CEO of Omada Health Grow His Company From Scratch | Inc.com https://www.inc.com/alexa-von-tobel/sean-duffy-omada-health-founders-project.html

9.5 Notes

____

____

____

____

____

____

Endnotes

1 About Omada Health https://www.omadahealth.com/about-us
2 Omada Health hits Unicorn status with $192M Fidelity-led Series E | Fierce Healthcare https://www.fiercehealthcare.com/health-tech/omada-health-hits-unicorn-status-192m-fidelity-led-series-e
3 https://pitchbook.com/
4 https://pitchbook.com/

Chapter 10

Redox

We solved our chicken-or-egg problem by building documentation for what our live product would (eventually) do. Then, to show there was real demand for it, we started charging developers to see the documentation.

Niko Skievaski, Co-founder and President

10.1 Quick Facts

Website	https://www.redoxengine.com/
Founded	2014
Mission	*Make Healthcare Data Useful* *As the leader in healthcare data interoperability, we provide providers, payers, and digital health organizations with the strongest data foundation for shifting to digital-first, value-based healthcare.*[1]
Founders	Niko Skievaski https://www.linkedin.com/in/skievaski/ Luke Bonney https://www.linkedin.com/in/luke-bonney-he-him-965a135/ James Lloyd, https://www.linkedin.com/in/jameslloyd608/

DOI: 10.4324/9781032711034-10

Unicorn status achieved	N/A*
Funding rounds[2]	Five funding deals • November 2014–January 2022 • Range from \$0.47 million in seed to \$45 million round
Leading funders from Series D round[3]	• .406 Ventures • RRE • Battery Ventures • Adams Street Partners

** While not a Unicorn, the Redox story was so compelling and unique, I thought it would be informative and useful for other digital health founders.*

10.2 TLDR

Ideate

- Founded by Niko Skievaski, Luke Bonney, and James Lloyd
- Focus on healthcare data interoperability
- Aim to help startups share data with Epic and other EHR systems
- Concept developed at 100health incubator
- Raised $350(k) from Angel Investors

Build

- Formed a team of six, including friends from Epic
- Participated in startup accelerator programs like Dreamit Health and Texas Medical Center
- Secured a letter of intent from Baylor for a multi-million, multi-year contract
- Raised funds from HealthX Ventures, .406 Ventures, RRE, Battery Ventures, and Adams Street
- Developed a cloud-based, multi-tenant tool
- Validated demand by charging for access to documentation

Launch

- First live customer: Gauss Surgical at Hackensack
- Pivoted business model to charge vendors instead of health systems
- Created viral cycles with vendors bringing Redox into more health systems and vice versa
- Raised Series A round, and revenue grew from documentation subscriptions and customer connections

Grow

- Participated in accelerators like Healthbox and Plug and Play
- Focused on community building and thought leadership
- Adopted *movement-based marketing* to promote better technology in healthcare
- Raised Series B and Series C funding rounds, increasing salaries and equity for employees
- Transitioned to microservices architecture for scalability

10.3 Meet the Founder

Niko Skievaski

Niko Skievaski is co-founder and CEO of Althea, a platform supporting the safe, accessible introduction of regulated psychedelics. He also founded the Forward Fund, which helps subsidize psychedelic care for those in need. A serial entrepreneur at the intersection of healthcare, technology, and mental health, Niko previously co-founded Redox, a leading healthcare data integration company. His work focuses on building systems that enable healing at scale, bridging entrepreneurship, healthcare, and impact to support the responsible growth of psychedelic therapy.

10.4 Interview with Niko Skievaski, Co-founder and President

I met both Luke and James, my co-founders, at Epic [the electronic medical records company]. We were all working there, and then I left Epic to start a different company, not Redox. We started the coworking space, 100state (https://100state.com/). James had also left Epic and joined 100state. The concept for 100state was for it to be a landing zone for people coming out of Epic and the university [University of Wisconsin], giving entrepreneurs a place where they could all gather, incubate ideas, and launch startups. It's important to note that with 10,000 employees, Epic is the biggest employer in Madison.

It was at 100state that James and I really started working together. We were both on the board, and the organization had a lot of different incubation-style activities. Then James and I founded 100health, which operated like a healthcare incubator. That's when we pulled in Luke, whom I convinced to leave Epic, to start 100health with us. So, the three of us started 100health, and we had a few companies in the incubator that were in the early stages of development. That's really when and where we came up with the idea for Redox.

We had to figure out why our incubator, 100health, was different from or better than other ones out there. We didn't know how to build companies because we had never done that. We were certain that we knew Epic technology really well, and we knew EHR technology at large. That knowledge led us down the path of asking ourselves if we could build infrastructure that would help a whole cohort of digital health companies.

It was James who came up with the idea because of his experience on the integration team at Epic. He realized that all these startup companies would have a problem sharing data with Epic, and he knew how to do it, at least once. And we can do it once for many companies with a single platform. That's where we got the idea behind Redox.

We were working on 100health, and Redox was just James' idea. We said to ourselves, "Ok, Redox is a company within 100health." Then we realized Redox is *the thing* that we think will actually make money. So, we moved it away from the incubator model, but 100health is still part of our story. In fact, 100health is still what our Slack channel is called, because that's what it was when we stood it up. Now, when a new person joins Redox, they always ask, "What is this 100health thing?" Vestiges of the incubator are still around in different places in our organization.

We also get asked about the name, and frankly, it was just what James called the project he was working on as part of 100health. We didn't go through some elaborate ideation about the name or anything. This was just what James called it, and by the time we ended up doing it, we were like, yeah, let's just call it Redox. It felt right because he got the name from chemistry, as in, there's a redox reaction. It causes rust, but it is a chemical reaction, and it's the molecules that are reacting by sharing electrons that go back and forth. So, in James' science-minded way, he thought, "Oh, this is what we are doing, enabling organizations to share data and create more value." And therein lies the chemistry. By the time we brought the product to market, we just said to ourselves, "Yep, it's just called Redox."

Not doing any real due diligence about the name came back to bite us later because the URL that we have is redoxengine.com, which confines us and makes us think of it as an interface engine. Even now, people will tell us that we are just an interface engine. However, we were trying to build a modern cloud-based version of an interface engine. I'm still a bit annoyed when people, even employees, call it the Redox Engine. I never say engine, despite the website URL.

Going back to our origin story, early on, we had the vision of helping startups in the digital health space. They don't know how to get data in and out of EHRs. We thought, OK, that's something we could fix. James knows how to do that. He knows how to move data from one place to another and has the vision of creating a platform to make it all work. This was the idea as we were coming out of Epic and seeing what was happening in digital health. Remember, this was late 2013, early 2014, when we were ideating, and digital health was growing, and everyone was talking about this new wave of technology. It was the time that the Internet was hitting healthcare, as Jonathan Bush [founder of Athena Health and also interviewed for this book in chapter 3] always used to put it. We were able to raise money from Angel Investors in Madison, who had seen Epic, but Epic didn't invest. The Angel Investors were high-net-worth individuals who looked at us as the next big Epic-type of thing. We raised $350(k), and Mark Bakken from HealthX Ventures led that round as an Angel Investor when he was still at Nordic Consulting, which prompted other Angel Investors to come in, too.

> ***Our plan in the first year was to get Redox live or to a point where we have enough evidence that it works and that we can raise more money.***

So, here we are – we have $350(k) and there are three of us. We then contacted three more friends we had at Epic – two developers and one on the business side. We formed a team of six, and if you do the math, the team of six splitting $350(k) doesn't go very far. The first year, I think we all paid ourselves about $25(k) for the whole year. Our plan in the first year was to get Redox live or to a point where we have enough evidence that it works and that we can raise more money.

Even at this point, we knew that to be successful, Redox would have to create network effects: if we have all the developers using it, then all the health systems will use it, and vice versa. We had this vision in our heads that we had to raise a lot of money and raise it sooner rather than later so we could grow faster to capture that market. From the beginning, we asked ourselves, "What are the milestones we need to hit to raise more money?" And that's literally how we ran the company from day one: what milestones do we need to hit to raise more money, and then, when we raise money, what milestones can we hit with this amount of money?

The $350(k) lasted for a year, and it was during this time that we did a bunch of startup accelerator programs. We went to Baltimore first and did Dreamit Health, which was partnered with Johns Hopkins. At this time, it's worth noting that we had this vision for Redox, but we still didn't know who our customer was or who was going to pay for it. But we thought we could move data between these two worlds.

Then we got buddied up with Johns Hopkins and the CIO there, which was a turning point for us. I remember printing the email because I knew this would be something we'd want to keep. It was an email from the CIO saying, "Yes, let's work with Redox," and she sent it to other people in the IT department, and we're ecstatic! "That's the golden ticket!"

We had won Hopkins; what else could we want? But selling to health systems is long and arduous, and even with this "golden ticket," it didn't go anywhere with Hopkins.

We worked with the Texas Medical Center accelerator with all the big health systems down there, and we had another one of those moments with Baylor. Baylor's CIO said that they wanted to essentially do all their integrations through us and that anything in the cloud should go through Redox. We got a letter of intent for a big contract, and we started designing the system. By this point, it's eight or so months in, and our engineering team of three engineers has been designing this whole thing to be in the cloud. Our vision was that this solution would be a cloud-based, multi-tenant tool.

But the one customer we had on the line was Baylor, and they came to us and wanted us to put Redox in their data center. Essentially, they wanted us to bring it down from the cloud, which prompted one of our early conflicts on the business side. At that moment, we are excited because we have this multi-million, multi-year contract, but our one customer wants it on-premise. Our developers are asking, "Why would we do that? The point of this is to be in the cloud."

We actually used that letter of intent from Baylor to help convince .406 Ventures to take us on.

We actually used that letter of intent from Baylor to help convince .406 Ventures to take us on. At least that's what we thought. We got a term sheet from .406 Ventures because they saw the Baylor letter of intent. The investors are convinced that the solution is actually going to work in health systems, and through that letter, they see that a reputable health system believes in us. We were all down in Houston, starting to do implementation work. Then the CIO got fired. He was our champion – the one who wanted to do all of this. And we don't even know he's been fired. He just never shows up for a meeting, and his team is like, "Hey, where is he?" We all start looking for him. And then we found out he was fired, and the whole deal was dead.

At this point, we had no revenue and no live customers. We did have an MVP, but we had to call .406 Ventures and say, "Hey, remember that letter of intent that we had? The deal is dead." We had a few months left of runway and thought, "[T]his is it, we're done." But, in an unexpected move, the partner at .406 Ventures, Liam Donohue, said, "You'll find another one. Don't worry about it."

And we're like, "Wait, what? That's incredible."

Our investors had a belief in our solution and who we were.

Looking back on it now, when we probed deeper with .406 Ventures about it, they had a thesis that a company like ours should exist. And when they met us, they agreed that we were the guys who were going to build it. So, it really didn't matter what contracts we may or may not have had. Our investors had a belief in our solution and who we were.

Going back a little bit before we were on this track of selling to health systems, we were participating in these accelerator programs, and in each of these accelerators, there are another ten companies that are all in digital health. All those founders knew that we were from Epic and would ask us, "How do I get the data?" And we replied, "That's what we are building!" We immediately saw this demand from startups and early-stage companies that have never gotten data in and out of EHRs before. They would come to us and ask how to do it.

We realized that there was rampant demand from these early-stage companies that had no money and no live customers. But they needed us, and we found ourselves having long conversations with them about how our solution worked, workflows, and how the data flowed.

This was our chicken-or-egg problem: startups needed our infrastructure at the health systems they were working with, but Redox wasn't installed at those health systems yet. We ended up advising these companies on how it would work to gather feedback. This turned into our developer documentation, explaining our API and how it would work.

> ***[I]f we charge them for the documentation, then it'll show that there's demand in the market.***

Then another conflict arose with our developers. James and I saw that all these developers loved our documentation. I wanted to charge for it. I want to put up a paywall in front of it, and James was opposed, pointing out that you would never charge developers for documentation; it's silly. But I was thinking, we can't charge them for our product because their solutions aren't deployed anywhere, and we can't help them go live faster, even though we are trying to. But if we charge them for the documentation, then it'll show that there's demand in the market. So, we started charging developers for this documentation. I would cold-call any CTO in the digital health space and say, "Hey, I used to work at Epic, and we can help you get your data and here's the documentation showing how to do it." And we had some development tools there, too. We ended up generating a couple of grand, about $5(k) of monthly recurring revenue, just from this paywall.

By the time we went to raise our Series A, we had that letter of intent from Baylor, and we had $5(k) of monthly recurring revenue from a *not-live* MVP documentation site. That was the evidence and market traction that enabled us to raise $3.5 million from .406 Ventures and Flybridge Capital. It was shortly after that, when one of the startups, Gauss Surgical, which was in our cohort at Texas Medical Center, got their first customer and needed Redox. Their solution was an iPad app that takes pictures of blood in the operating room to more accurately measure blood loss. But the startup had no idea how to get that data into the EHR or even know who the patient was while being operated on in the operating room.

Gauss Surgical's first customer was Hackensack, in New Jersey, and we came in as the startup's integration team, showing how the integration worked. We implemented their product through Redox, resulting in a signed BAA with the health system. We transferred the data into their platform, running their solution through our technology, and that was our first live customer. We acted as an outsourced implementation consultant, so we didn't have to go through sales and procurement with Hackensack ourselves.

Gauss paid us $500 a month for that connection, which was our standard pricing at the time. With this project, we saw our first live data.

> ***We don't charge the health system, but we charge the vendor, which totally accelerated growth for us then and today.***

Before this, in our talks with Hopkins, Baylor, and other health systems, we had always thought the health system would pay. But we realized that it took the startup, Gauss Surgical, so long to get their customer, Hackensack, to figure out how to pay them that we knew that we didn't want to charge Hackensack and have to go through contracting and all of that arduous procurement process. Fortunately, Gauss said that they would pay us out of what they were getting paid from Hackensack. It was that experience that led us to our business model, which is still the business model Redox has today. We don't charge the health system, but we charge the vendor, which totally accelerated growth for us then and today. We pivoted from selling into the health system's IT department, which is where so many people get stuck. Instead, we sold to the developers and helped the developers solve the health system's problem. As a result, the health systems have become a partner for us. In this case, we are live at Hackensack and have created a relationship with them and their integration team. We are up and running and have patient health information going through our systems. Once that relationship was cemented, we were able to go back to the integration team at Hackensack and say, "What other projects do you have coming along? We can use the same connection for anything in the cloud." The strategy worked, as Hackensack would send vendors they were doing business with, and we would onboard those vendors as customers as well.

In this approach, Hackensack gets the value, but we don't have to contract directly with them. Often, we will tell the vendor that they can pay us $500 a month, or they can do it themselves with Hackensack, but that would likely take them like six months longer, and they'd have to manage every connection on their own. The value proposition becomes a no-brainer for the vendors, in addition to Hackensack.

We essentially had two viral cycles emerge to help Redox grow:

1. Vendors bringing us into more health systems
2. Health systems bringing us to more vendors

The result was a network effect that shaped our business model and early growth.

At the same time we went live, we raised our Series A round, and revenue was about $5(k)/month from our documentation subscriptions (which we ended up making free after the Series A), plus the one customer of $500 per month.

> ***[B]uilding a community gave us the opportunity to know people, understand the problems, connect them with each other.***

From that point on, when we participated in accelerators, the main thing for us was building a community, which brought customers to us. We did a lot of tactical things right, too, but building community gave us the opportunity to know people, understand the problems, and connect them with each other. In fact, it was the Dreamit Accelerator that introduced us to .406 Ventures and Flybridge, who ended up investing in the Series A.

We found so much value in the DreamIt Accelerator, and we really liked their focus. We all moved to Baltimore, and then we moved to Houston for the Texas Medical Center Accelerator – things I could only imagine doing in my 20s, before kids, responsibilities, and other stuff. Both programs really helped us focus while building meaningful relationships with our customers. I am still friends with people from the other accelerator companies. Some of them were successful and have even moved on to other companies. It's such a small ecosystem in health tech, but we found that accelerators were a great way to build community in the region.

After our time in Baltimore, we were convinced that we had a good handle on the market on the East Coast, and we moved on to Houston. In the Texas Medical Accelerator, they taught us to say they have the biggest medical center in the world. They do have a big community down there, and they had us pitch multiple times to all the different health systems there, building our name and brand.

> ***At this time, I was also writing a lot on our blog, sharing our experiences about working on the startup side of digital health after coming from the Epic side of the industry. I think that writing actually helped to build more community and more trust, because I was very candid.***

Then we did the Healthbox accelerator with Intermountain Health, and we did the Plug and Play accelerator in the Bay Area. Each of these programs was an opportunity for us to immerse ourselves not only with the other startup founders in the program, who were our peers, but with the local health systems as well. We wanted to help the health systems that needed to trust us to implement. At this time, I was also writing a lot on our blog, sharing our experiences about working on the startup side of digital health after coming from the Epic side of the industry. I think that writing actually helped to build more community and more trust because I was very candid. I would share that we didn't know what we were doing all the time while sharing some of the problems we saw.

We were also tracking the adoption of cloud-based technologies. All these new vendors were building applications in the cloud while the health systems were trying not to do anything in the cloud. I talked to a lot of CIOs and IT people about that and ended up writing for HIStalk [a healthcare IT news and opinion website, https://histalk2.com/] for a while. Through this thought leadership and community building, we had stumbled upon what I started calling *movement-based marketing*. There was a bigger mission that we were all working toward – to have better technology in healthcare. Redox was part of the mission-building, trying to remove interoperability as a barrier, as a sort of rallying cry for the movement.

And we still feel that today. I was on LinkedIn the other day and saw the Epic/First Particle health story. [Following a month-long dispute, data platform Particle Health sued EHR behemoth Epic. The startup filed an antitrust lawsuit against Epic in the Southern District of New York on Monday, alleging that the EHR vendor is using its dominance in the market to prevent competition in the payer platform space.[4]]

I see the relics of our mission in these new arguments for better interoperability. In the beginning, back in 2014 and 2015, when we were emerging, people were rooting for us because we were focused on trying to unlock the healthcare data trapped in EMRs. We found that it was easy to get on stages, participate in panels, write articles, and contribute to the larger industry conversation because there was momentum in the health tech community. I felt like I needed to be the champion of this movement and represent what it meant.

> ***[I]t created a culture in our company that felt very mission-driven even though we were three or four steps removed from actual patient care.***

As a result, it created a culture in our company that felt very mission-driven, even though we were three or four steps removed from actual patient care.

It felt like we were doing this to save healthcare in America. Everyone has a healthcare story, and that motivated us; our mission influenced the way we delivered our product to customers.

> ***It is just clear talking to you guys that you give a sh*t and that you care about this work. And I can trust you because of that.***

We got to the point where we were asking customers to come to team meetings so we could hear their stories and pick their brains about all sorts of things. I remember we had one customer tell us why he liked working with us: "It is just clear talking to you guys that you give a sh*t and that you care about this work. And I can trust you because of that."

And so from that moment, "[g]iving a shit" became one of our mottos and one of our core values in the company. It also became the guiding light in how we work with customers. Anyone in digital health is doing it, most likely, or because they are also mission-driven, because they have had some experience, or they understand the impact that it has. Redox gets to live vicariously through that.

To this day, all our customer-facing people embody that attitude and mission focus.

> ***We paid everyone the same amount until we raised our Series C funding.***

In the early days, this mission-driven approach really set our culture and management style. We paid everyone the same amount until we raised our Series C funding. And that salary was below market. At our Angel round, everyone got paid $25(k) for the first year. And then we raised our Series A, and we wanted to hire more people, but 3.5 million doesn't last that long either. At that point, I think the salary was about $40(k) or $50(k) for everyone in the company. We were hiring people coming out of Epic who were making $250(k) or $300(k) as developers and giving them a platform to solve the problem they wanted to solve at Epic. We paid them very badly, but we also paid ourselves badly and were purposely transparent about it. Making it equal worked because we [the founders] could say, "I make that much too. Everyone here does." Employees couldn't ask for more because we were all earning the same amount. Instead, everyone knew we were in this together and doing this for the movement. We were revolutionaries, not employees.

> ***But there was also an upside for members of our team, as we overcompensated in equity.***

But there was also an upside for members of our team, as we *overcompensated* in equity. After the Series A round, we carved out a bigger-than-normal option pool, and we gave people more equity than you'd probably typically get at an early-stage company, coming in as employee 10, 11, or 20. We wanted people to really feel ownership, and so it was a very, very mission-oriented company and team.

It's funny because that approach segmented the types of people who could work at Redox. One category was young people just coming out of college, who were like, "$40(k), whatever. I can make that work. It's more than the zero I was making before." These were hustling types, and some of them are still at Redox to this day. (One person is now leading business development, and his whole career has been at Redox, which is awesome.)

But then on the other side of it, we had people who could afford not to make money for a little while. And so it was that contrast – there was no one in the middle who actually needed money to survive. Well, the younger people did, but they didn't have expenses.

We were getting these developers, and they were largely coming out of Epic because that was our network. We eventually started hiring people, especially from the Bay Area, who wanted to get out of that rat race and move somewhere. Redox was, and still is, a fully remote company, allowing new hires to live wherever they want.

We hired people who could afford to take a risk. In response, our commitment to them was, every time we raise more money and hit more milestones, we're going to raise pay, which we ended up doing after the Series B. We were then making $80(k), and we all felt rich! When we closed our Series C, we actually started getting more serious about having an HR function and creating teams with salary bands and more traditional benefits.

> ***Even to this day we have a philosophy around paying people: the 50th percentile for salary, based on the data out there for that role, but then the 90th percentile in equity. We still want to overcompensate on the equity side.***

Even to this day, we have a philosophy around paying people: the 50th percentile for salary, based on the data out there for that role, but then the 90th percentile in equity. We still want to overcompensate on the equity side. Like I said earlier, we tried to sell to enterprises, like Baylor [Scott and White], and what's funny is that none of those organizations ever said "no." I think that's one of the most challenging parts about healthcare enterprise sales.

> ***You never get a "no" from a customer. They will just drag you on forever. Time is your most valuable resource. Getting a "no" is rare and a gift; otherwise the never-ending sales process can kill a company.***

You never get a "no" from a customer. They will just drag you on forever. Time is your most valuable resource. Getting a "no" is rare and a gift; otherwise, the never-ending sales process can kill a company. We were getting dragged through the whole pipeline of enterprise sales processes because when I left Epic, I had a good understanding of who the customers were. We were getting meetings with IT teams, and they could trust us because we had worked on their projects, but it was so hard to close a deal.

Meanwhile, we're working with startups, and we figured out that startups are so much more fun to work with, and we didn't charge them until they went live. It was like we were investing in the startups, saying, "We want you to get live and if you get live, you get paid and then you pay us." This is how it worked at the beginning. (But that's not how Redox does it today, as we charge upfront, which I'm a bit bitter about.) We wanted to invest alongside these startups and help them try to figure out how to make that business model work.

> ***The thing that differentiates us from people who simply solve the consumers' or startups' problems or are focused on a less robust or durable market is that, when those startup customers went live at the health system, we now also had relationship with the health system, which was real.***

The thing that differentiates us from people who simply solve the consumers' or startups' problems or are focused on a less robust or durable market is that, when those startup customers went live at the health system, we now also had a relationship with the health system, which was real. We literally had a VPN tunnel into their data center. We had signed a BAA [Business Associates Agreement], and we had done something that the health system was impressed by because we made their integration project go much faster. Typically, the customer and digital health company would talk past each other. But we would come in and say "[T]his is what we are going to do and then go live."

The connection to the health system was really helpful because some of the startups didn't make it out of pilot mode and would fail. There was a little more churn with the early-stage startups, which you would expect. But the relationships with the health system would remain intact. In fact, they would tell us who else they were working with, and some of those vendors were bigger companies, which helped us climb up the company size ladder to mid-market and eventually enterprise-size digital health companies. That led to a ramping up and acceleration of those viral cycles because enterprise companies have bigger markets that they were selling into.

From a technology side, we didn't have a premeditated choice for our cloud vendor, as our first three developers, James, Nick, and TC, all came out of Epic, which is on-prem and built on Massachusetts General Hospital Utility Multi-Programming System and Caché. You can't build on that technology to this day, especially in the cloud.

I don't know how they made the decisions that they did, but I know that there was a lot of thought that went into it, and a lot of rework went into it as well. TC (Christopher Tobin Campbell, but the Tobin Campbell part is TC, and that's what everyone calls him) became our chief architect and still is. He is the mastermind behind how all the infrastructure works together.

Redox processes hundreds of millions of messages every day, generating a lot of throughput that needs to happen in real time without things going down. If our system goes down, patient lives are on the line. Therefore, there was a lot of thought that went into the cloud architecture. There were at least three distinct times when we would come back on a Monday, and TC would announce that he had rebuilt the whole thing over the weekend, and we needed to move everything over to the new system. He had found a better way, and that new way was the development project for the week.

TC is one of those one in a million developers where he would just get an idea in his head, and he would have to build it. The development team was super thoughtful about things, and it was just so fun watching the collaboration between the developers. Then I would pop in and ask, "Hey, customers are asking for this. Is this possible?" And then they would say, "In a week." And I'm thinking to myself, SWEET!

We ended up using AWS. All our developers have to take the basic AWS training and stuff like that. At some point, we switched to React [an open-source library for web and native user interface].[5] There are a lot of technical decisions that change over time. TypeScript [TypeScript is a strongly typed programming language that builds on JavaScript, giving you better tooling at any scale][6] was a newer thing that we adopted.

(For any developers who read this portion, they'll roll their eyes because this is not my cup of tea.)

One of the biggest technical challenges that I have only come to appreciate in hindsight, were the tradeoffs between building fast and building for scale.

One of the biggest technical challenges that I have only come to appreciate in hindsight was the trade-offs between building fast and building for scale. I think that's why TC is probably one of the most brilliant engineers that I know, because he can achieve that balance. I feel like some engineers start with the idea that they are going to build it the right way, for the scale that they someday hope to reach, and then there are some engineers who are scrappy, building it fast to get it done.

The whole culture changed at that moment because we knew this was important.

When we first went live at Hackensack, we watched the first data come through our platform. We started asking, "What is that number that is being transmitted?" Then we realized it was the blood loss by mothers during emergency cesarean sections. And we were like, oh, wow! They're measuring blood loss in a live operating room with a baby and a mom. That's when it really hit us: if Redox goes down, the clinicians don't see that [the blood loss measurement]. The whole culture changed at that moment because we knew this was important. We enabled one type of integration with that project, but then the next five integrations were different styles of integrations. Our engineering team had to think about building a platform that was extendable to a wide range of integrations and data types that we would need to move. We also needed to support established workflows while also being fast enough to support the random things our customers were requesting. This is why TC found himself rebuilding it on the weekends – he would get to a point where he was certain that it couldn't scale much further, and then he'd have to build another version that could scale more effectively.

Three years ago, we moved to a microservices architecture, which was a huge project, leading to another entire rebuild of everything. The result is now we are now much more scalable, and there's not a single point of failure. Each part can be thought of as a scalable piece rather than this behemoth thing. What was so challenging about this was when we needed to rebuild things, we'd have to move all these VPNs, which required us to call the health system and have them change the port that they're sending the data to.

Now, Redox has thousands and thousands of VPNs, but at the time, even if we had 100, we'd have to call 100 health systems and submit a ticket to IT. Then they would update the port, and we'd have to test it – every time we did a rebuild, we had to do stuff like that. It was challenging for sure, but it was all resolved once we moved to the microservices architecture.

I think one of the reasons we frequently made the right decision was the culture we had among our founders.

There were a lot of decisions that we made in the moment that we had no idea would be so important. But as I look back, I realize we could have done so much worse. It just so happened that we made the right decisions. I think one of the reasons we frequently made the right decision was the culture we had among our founders. There are three of us: I was the go-to-market guy talking to customers; James was our technology guy; and Luke was our operational guy, running the company, ensuring that we had the right conversations. That made Luke the manager of everybody, and whenever the decision came up that needed us to all agree, we could argue really well. Most of the time, we had full consensus, but sometimes it was two-to-one, and we could *disagree and commit.* If I were the one who disagreed, I could still commit because I trusted my co-founders. I think that was really helpful because it forced us to have conversations and come up with frameworks for how to make decisions.

If a customer needed an on-premise solution, we knew that we were not the vendor for that customer. We had made the decision that we were not the vendor to solve that problem. Those decisions gave us a lane in which to focus, and made it really clear how and when we were going to work with customers.

For example, our decision to not go on-prem with any technology was partly due to the market conditions at that time, but also because of what we learned when the Baylor CIO was fired. We really struggled with that decision, and it was me versus James, and Luke was the one trying to help us find the balance. We ended up in the cloud, and that became a boundary for us. We agreed that we were not going to put anything on premise. If a customer needed an on-premise solution, we knew that we were not the vendor for that customer. We had made the decision that we were not the vendor to solve that problem. Those decisions gave us a lane in which to focus and made it really clear how and when we were going to work with customers.

I didn't know how important those decisions were at the time. But what it came down to was having a great relationship with my co-founders and none of us having an ego about it.

Other major decisions included which investors to work with, and I think we were incredibly lucky with .406 Ventures. The story that I mentioned earlier exemplified their trust in us as leaders of the company. Essentially, it was important that we picked investors who understood the long-term vision of the company and the reason why we were doing it. This enabled us to all be aligned to the long-term view and agree when and how to raise money. I didn't know how important those decisions were at the time. But what it came down to was having a great relationship with my co-founders and none of us having an ego about it. Also, we stayed very company-oriented, always focused on the best thing for the company. Even early on, we decided that all three of us as founders would have the same vesting schedule as everyone else, which is not very common. A lot of founders are focused on maximizing their own equity. But we were aware that if I need to leave in a year, I can't take a third of the company with me; that would kill the company.

Stepping back a moment, currently, we have customers that are startups as well as larger organizations. After achieving product-market fit on the startup side, I formed a small team and went back and tried to sell directly to health systems, as they were receiving value too. How can we extract value and revenues from the providers?

We worked for two years straight, pitching to health systems, and got three deals. But they were with innovation groups at health systems, and the projects were within those innovation departments. Our goal was to have the health system select us as their modern interface engine, and we never got there. There are interface engines that health systems can buy, but we could never get them to buy our solution as a cloud-based interface engine. Perhaps it was due to my lack of enterprise sales experience. Looking back, perhaps someone could have sold more successfully, but we never got product-market fit with health systems. To this day, I think only about 3%–4% of our revenue comes directly from health systems.

One of the most challenging things about selling to health systems (and why we never wanted to scale any of those models) is that healthcare IT teams are used to getting what they want because they are spending lots of money. Providers' IT teams expect high levels of customization and weekly meetings with their teams. It was like they wanted us to be part of their team. We were flying to their offices all the time, and we realized that it was just not as scalable as what we were doing for the startups and vendors.

We had much more product-led growth with the vendor side. We still aspire to working with big enterprises that need a lot of customization, and that's why our pricing has changed. Instead of one product, we hired a product marketing team that broke it into four products. Frankly, I never learned what the four products were because to me it's the same old thing. But that's what product marketing does – they identified four values and customer segments, and now we charge differently for all of them, even though the individual products don't really work independently.

> ***Figuring out how to get user feedback early on is super important, and I think our MVP at Redox accomplished that.***

In working with startups, we saw a lot of people spend a lot of time and money building a fully baked product before they had users. There is justification for doing that, especially in healthcare, when lives are on the line and things like that. But having feedback from real, live users is more important than anything. I would take calls from startups that didn't have any live customers, and they would like to demo their product for me. I saw beautiful products with features galore. And they had no idea if anyone wanted to use it. Figuring out how to get user feedback early on is super important, and I think our MVP at Redox accomplished that. Selling our documentation enabled us to get feedback on how it would work if people were using it, which was super important.

> ***I guess what I'm trying to say is to make sure you are getting feedback from those customers, ensuring they absolutely love your product before you start turning on the scaling machine.***

I guess what I'm trying to say is to make sure you are getting feedback from those customers, ensuring they absolutely love your product before you start turning on the scaling machine. Scaling is very, very costly. We've seen a lot of companies that raised a lot of money with a big valuation but can't hit the milestones in the two years of runway that the round buys them. Then they find themselves doing a down-round or having to lay people off.

> ***I think protecting that winning energy is imperative, and that doesn't mean lying to employees or anything. It means making the choices to set you up for success.***

There's this winning energy that you can feel from companies that are crushing it. They look at every obstacle as an opportunity. And you can feel the momentum, the flow of the organization. But when you get over your skis, lay people off, don't meet your numbers, and do a down round, it feels bad and feels like the company is losing energy. There are companies we talk to that just feel beaten up from whatever traumas they've encountered along the way. I think protecting that winning energy is imperative, and that doesn't mean lying to employees or anything. It means making the choices to set you up for success.

I think Redox was always very reasonable with how much we raised and the valuations so that we could have a good round the next time. We took a lot of dilution, knowing that if this thing works, it's going to be huge. For us, it was sort of binary. If I own a small percentage of a huge thing, I'm still rich, so it doesn't matter how much equity I own in the company.

I'm able to relate all of this to my cycling. There's a saying in cycling that it [cycling] doesn't get easier; you just get faster. The pro cyclists are in just as much pain as the commuter climbing the hill on the way to work. I think about that in the startup experience. So much of it is really hard early on. Then you get traction, you get funding and start working, and you have product-market fit. But it doesn't get easier; you just get faster, and the impact is bigger. More lives are on the line – your employees, your customers, all of that. The stakes get higher.

> ***That means you have to protect yourself in that process and have boundaries and make sure you're aware of the sacrifices you're making.***

Founders, I think, often look for the light at the end of the tunnel. They think that if they can just get through this next milestone, it's going to be easier – if they can just raise the money or just get the next round. In some cases, that's true, but that's just the roller coaster of the ride. It's always hard. That means you have to protect yourself in that process and have boundaries and make sure you're aware of the sacrifices you're making.

You should write them down.

You should know about them.

You should talk to your partner about them.

You should consciously choose these sacrifices and trade-offs. Otherwise, you burn out which causes that *loss of energy*. Looking back at the Redox experience, it was fun. It was very fun the whole time. It seems so many startups are not fun, or they only talk about the sacrifices and challenges.

I think it was fun largely because of the culture we created and the people that we got to work with throughout the process. It's also about the industry and the impact we are making. If you're not having fun, then there's something wrong – that's a signal that something's wrong. This should be the best job you ever have because you get to make it yourself. Throughout the journey, I have always been appreciative, even when things become difficult. I focus my gratitude meditation on this amazing opportunity I have. And I think that permeates throughout the culture, from founders to the entire team.

10.5 Notes

Endnotes

1 Company | Redox (redoxengine.com)
2 PitchBook Profile – Redox.
3 https://my.pitchbook.com/profile/81817-48/company/profile#deal-history
4 Unpacking the Epic-Particle Health Dispute: When It Started, What's Being Alleged & What It Means for the Industry – MedCity News.
5 React website.
6 TypeScript: JavaScript With Syntax For Types. website.

Chapter 11

Recurring Themes and Wisdom

Well, you've come this far, hearing from very exceptional and driven founders. Are you inspired, energized, and ready to take on the world of healthcare? I hope so! While you ruminate over the founders' journeys, I want to share common themes and potential actions you can take as a founder.

11.1 Themes

Every founder story is unique; however, key elements of their journeys are worth highlighting as foundational factors that, if implemented, could improve your likelihood of long-term success. These elements are leadership, market research, business development, customer relationships, regulatory compliance, data privacy and security, mentorship and guidance, and innovative strategies.

11.1.1 Leadership

The leaders I interviewed were humble and showed a servant-style of leadership. I think we all have images of founders in the Steve Jobs mode – tyrannical, mercurial, and brilliant. These founders, while also brilliant, were more apt to be collaborative and uniformly played down the Unicorn moniker. They celebrated the milestone, but the celebrations were often

DOI: 10.4324/9781032711034-11

short-lived or considered to be more important for the corporate culture and those working behind the scenes. Impacting patients was much more important to these founders than any valuation or other superficial milestone. Additionally, the founders seem informed about their competitors but not obsessed with them. Competitive pressures were handled by building value and acknowledging that there is enough work for everyone in this industry.

I also noticed an emphasis on balancing long-term goals and near-term planning. Many spoke of keeping the big goal on the horizon while achieving meaningful interim milestones every 3–6 months. (Which is why I'm not a fan of "moon shots," but that's a topic for another day.) I think Redox's story is a great example of improvising to generate revenue while working on the ultimate solution. Innovaccer's approach to hiring, emphasizing the importance of hiring people who would fit into roles two years from now, not only was unique but also showed a clear understanding of how to balance near- and long-term goals in building their team.

Another balancing act that founders found difficult to navigate dealt with burn rate, expenditures, and how to be good stewards of their investors' funds. Interestingly, in this group of founders, being too frugal seemed to be more prevalent. There were times that a few of the founders – in an effort to save money – ended up thwarting progress by spending too little. This was particularly evident in the story about Element Biosciences first office space.

Lastly, many of them talked about fun, joy, and excitement. When they spoke about their companies, colleagues, customers, and products, their eyes lit up, smiles were ever-present, and I got the sense that they *loved* their work. However, most of them were also not satisfied with resting on their laurels. Many described the work yet to be done, plans for future products, and additional ways they plan to continue improving healthcare.

11.2 Market Research

In my own *non-scientific* research, I often find that one of the most overlooked areas of building a company is market research. Or worse, the market research is conducted but flawed with overstated total addressable market statistics and exaggerated penetration figures. However, that was not the case with these Unicorns. All the founders conducted some sort of research to hone their mission and products. It was interesting to learn how many of the Unicorns identified "proxy customers,"[1] to give them feedback on their products, becoming *actual* customers later.

In the case of athenahealth, their market research was conducted while building another type of business. Instead of building a set of birthing clinics staffed with midwives, they started building the billing system for those clinics, which then became athenahealth, a medical records and billing company. Aidoc founder Elad Walach mentioned being "obsessed" with their customers, remaining engaged with the customers to understand how they were using the product and what improvements were needed. Element Biosciences built a solution that met the needs of customers overlooked by the incumbent. It was only through understanding the current market conditions that they could establish their unique value proposition. In the case of DispatchHealth, their research took the form of utilization metrics, costs of patient care, and other key indicators. But then their real market research began when they started teaming up with local emergency services organizations and staffing them with advanced nurse practitioners or PAs.

11.3 Business Development

Naivete was also a common theme. Boldness and enough ego to think, "I can solve this," were often met with unforeseen obstacles and surprises about just how difficult it would be to build and sell a solution in healthcare. Whether it was regulatory obstacles, technical challenges, or finding the right team, building the business was not a linear process. Lunit's story about starting in retail and then pivoting into healthcare is a good example of this. It was only through their direct involvement with regulators that they understood and shaped the regulations they would later comply with. Furthermore, Amwell and DispatchHealth had to overcome the morass of dealing with practitioner licensing requirements, which vary from state to state.

I expected to learn about the regulatory and technical challenges that many founders encountered, but I was surprised by the go-to-market difficulties (which may be my own personal bias as a long-time business developer). "Build it and they will come" was a common misconception. Frankly, this is a common refrain with founders at all stages, and I've spoken to more than a few who have assumed that by building a good product, customers will just come knocking on your door. The long-term effect of this is that the development of the GTM strategy often lags behind product development, causing sales and marketing teams to be hired later than they should. Another issue is having the CEO or other C-level executive try to run the sales and marketing programs. There are two issues with this approach: (1) Usually, the executive is too busy to dedicate the time needed to be successful and close deals, and (2) nothing SCREAMS "we are a startup" more than having the CEO or other non-business development leader work with customers and prospects. It signals that the startup is not fully staffed and ready to execute.

I was also surprised by the enduring business mantra that was popular in the 1980s, "No one ever got fired for buying IBM." While no longer the case since the technology industry has changed so much, it does point to the need for startups to understand the intricacies of building a brand. These days, it may not be IBM that a startup is up against, but one of the big cloud vendors or the myriads of solution providers and systems integrators. Furthermore, building a brand has many more aspects to it than in the 1980s. With social media, podcasts, webinars, conferences, and AI-generated content now in the mix, branding is both democratized and highly complex. All too often, startups fail to emphasize the importance of brand building or fail to build their brand as they try too many communications channels all at once, instead of doing the research needed to find which channels their prospects use and, therefore, are likely to be most effective.

You won't like this last one – plain dumb luck. It seems true that serendipity does play a role in achieving key milestones along the way to Unicorn status. However, it's incumbent upon the founders and their trusted advisors to be open-minded so that those moments of serendipity are identified and maximized. I'm a big believer in the ability to make opportunities come alive by paying attention, staying focused on your goals, and being able to recognize when circumstances enable you to achieve something you thought impossible.

11.4 Customer Relationships

To me, as a career business developer, how these Unicorns cultivated customers is especially fascinating. And let's be clear – truly connecting with customers in a meaningful and value-driven way can make or break an early-stage company (or enterprise, for that matter). Furthermore, the old adage, "You can only make a first impression once," is even more critical in the early days of a startup. In this group of Unicorns, there was a consistent goal of making *their customers* successful – not focusing on their own success.

Omada Health's decision to wait until the third version of their product before launching showed a tremendous amount of restraint and a laser focus on their ultimate goal. This resulted in going to market with a product that people actually wanted and were willing to buy. They had spent an enormous amount of time talking to patients and prospective customers, so by the time they got to V3 of their product, the customers were ready to buy a solution that was designed to specifically meet their needs.

Redox had the most innovative approach to building a pipeline of prospective customers by charging developers for their product documentation as Redox built their solution. Not only was it an early indicator of demand for their product, but it also cemented relationships and trust with their customers. In all my years of business development, this has to be one of the most innovative approaches to generating early revenue and building a customer base.

But not all customer relationships have to be direct. I'm a big fan of finding distributors or partners for joint GTM activities. Lunit's partnership with Fujifilm was a game-changer for them. Fortunately, the Lunit team had the forethought to host a demo site on their website that Fujifilm could test for themselves! Additionally, Amwell worked with partners to scale their solution, essentially white-labeling their services to organizations like Optum/UHG and WellPoint (now Anthem/Elevance) to spark their growth. At Omada Health, their initial customers were referrals from medical directors or people inside a plan, employer, or health system who were struggling to deal with the onslaught of patients. After showing helpful data from their prototype, these clinicians became the referral engine to others in their organizations.

11.5 Regulatory Compliance

We all understand why the regulations are so important in healthcare, but no one likes dealing with them or enjoys trying to navigate the web of complicated compliance requirements. Most founders first need to understand what regulations apply to their solution, and then they have to find someone to help them comply with them. While not the case with these founders, I have spoken to many early-stage founders who invested a ton of money in a "regulatory expert," who turned out not to be, costing the founder valuable time in terms of product and go-to-market roadmaps, in addition to the outlay of precious capital.

Lunit's experience helping to engineer the regulations in South Korea was both unique and pivotal in helping them build their product. Few founders today will find themselves in a similar situation. However, as we continue to integrate AI into systems and solutions, the regulatory landscape will evolve – perhaps faster than ever. This is overwhelming, and yet it presents an opportunity, as government agencies seek input from key stakeholders. In the United States, the FDA publishes new draft regulations, typically seeking industry comments. For example, in December of 2024, the FDA posted "Marketing Submission Recommendations for a Predetermined Change Control Plan (PCCP) for Artificial Intelligence-Enabled Device Software Functions,"[2] which enabled anyone to submit their thoughts on the draft PCCP guidance. While this may be a bit more than a founder would like to take on, founders can ensure that their point of view is represented through working with *reputable* regulatory consultants and experts or joining consortiums like the Coalition for Healthcare AI or CHAI (https://chai.org/). At a minimum, founding teams need to understand what laws and regulations will apply to them. For example, ConcertAI knew that they had to manage a variety of regulations from HHS, HIPAA, and FDA, which provide guardrails for running clinical trials and handling personal health information.

11.5.1 Data Security and Privacy

As the attack surface continues to grow across all industries, including healthcare, security and privacy become table stakes. Failing to handle patient data securely and ensure privacy has been the downfall of more than one company. Most of us are very familiar with the Change Healthcare hack in February 2024, which exposed the data of 100 million patients, making it the largest US healthcare data breach to date.[3] Perhaps one of the most important lessons that founders should take away from this (besides being absolutely certain that you are maintaining a sound cybersecurity posture) is that this breach was from a third-party company. It wasn't UHG that was hacked – it was the third-party company working with UHG. Furthermore, the ripple effect was pronounced. "hundreds of thousands of physician practices, hospitals, and pharmacies were unable to submit claims or receive payments. With the weeks-long paralysis and ponderous shift to alternative protocols, many facilities found themselves unable to deliver care and facing financial collapse."[4] No one wants to be "that company" that shuts down operations – literally and figuratively.

Fortunately, and uniformly, the Unicorns profiled in this book that deal with patient data are committed to ensuring data is safeguarded and handled in accordance with best practices and regulations. This means ensuring patient and user consent, anonymizing data, using synthetic data, and partnering with organizations like HITRUST, which "has championed programs that safeguard sensitive information and manage information risk for global organizations across industries and throughout the third-party supply chain."[5] Amwell, athenahealth, ConcertAI, DispatchHealth, Innovaccer, Omada Health, and Redox are all HITRUST-certified. While the certification process isn't easy or quick, it's very helpful in maintaining a strong security stance, especially as the nature of cyberattacks continues to evolve.

11.6 Mentorship and Guidance

[Side note: Jonathan Bush, founder of athenahealth, is a mentor to Abhinav Shashank, founder of Innovaccer. Don't you love how connected we all are?]

Effective mentors and advisors can make a huge difference in the trajectory of a company, and this fact was not lost on the founders. The Unicorn founders often had outside advisors or mentors who supported their journey. Lunit's journey from retail to healthcare was driven by guidance from their medical school friends, who later became radiologists and became their first customers. Abhinav Shashank of Innovaccer, Sean Duffy of Omada Health, and Elad Walach of Aidoc all emphasized the importance of having a mentor. Abhinav noted that he had two mentors – one to help him understand the healthcare industry (Jonathan Bush) and one for the financial side (Sumir Chadha from WestBridge Capital). Sean Duffy specifically noted that his mentors changed as Omada Health grew. It was important to him that his mentors had similar experiences and could help him guide the company to the next major milestone. This is an interesting concept, as many of us think of mentors as people who will stand by us throughout the process. Have you changed mentors as you have grown and changed?

11.7 Innovative Strategies

When I first conjured up the idea for this book, I had no idea just how many ways innovation can take shape. The ten Unicorns described in this book all took very different path from each other and from others in their segments. As mentioned earlier, Redox's early business model to sell their documentation was highly innovative and unlike traditional business development strategies. In addition, standardizing the pay across all positions in the early days was also unique and really set the tone for their corporate culture. The demo site that Lunit posted to their website was also quite interesting and helped them land their biggest partnership (Fujifilm) at that time. We often talk about freemium options in this industry, but Lunit's self-serve demo site is something altogether different and may be worth emulating if it fits your business model.

ConcertAI's approach to building its customer base was not unlike buying into the options market. They were selling their future product, with customers taking on an obligation to pay for it once they delivered and met acceptance criteria. This approach may not be feasible for all, but if you have the credibility and track record (and financial acumen and systems to track it), this could be an interesting way to initiate early revenue streams.

Few companies that I've known or have worked with have been as purposeful in taking on the incumbent as Element Biosciences. Their mission was to democratize DNA sequencing by taking on Illumina, a Unicorn itself and industry leader. Element's ability to identify a gap between high-throughput Illumina and smaller, low-throughput challengers enabled them to build a strategy and company based on the best of both, identifying and then filling a much-needed niche in the industry while preparing them to pursue new market segments.

athenahealth started in a very different business – maternity clinics. But the innovator mindset enabled the founding team to understand that what they had built, a medical records and billing system, was actually their best way of bringing value to the industry. Not unlike Lunit, they started with one mission and ended up delivering a solution and a company that leveraged the work they had done, but in a completely new way.

I also found Innovaccer's approach to hiring to be quite intriguing. It takes guts and confidence to adopt a hiring strategy like theirs that hires people for what they will become. It's hard enough to find the right people you need today, much less to project what skills they will bring to the organization two years from now. However, the foresight and strategic planning required to successfully hire the right team members for today and the future should be considered by startups at all stages. If you are building financial and sales forecasts, developing a product roadmap, and building GTM strategies, why not also build a longer-term hiring and personnel plan?

Redox also had an innovative approach when it came to running the company. The three founders decided that vigorous disagreements were allowed and even welcomed, but once the debate was over, the rules of engagement required them to agree to disagree but commit to whatever course of action won the two-to-one majority. Operating this way takes a lot of humility and trust, helping them build a decision-making framework and leading them to become a market leader.

11.8 Next Steps: Your Action Plan

At this point, I hope you are brimming with new ideas and inspiration to build your own business. Going back to the Ideate, Build, Launch, and Grow model that served as the foundation for The Startup Protocol and this book, here are some things for you to consider based on what we learned from these Unicorn founders:

Ideate

- Get input from proxy customers often and at every stage to help keep you focused on building a solution that people will buy.
- Remain open to pivoting as market forces and other key factors lead you in other directions.
- Ensure your mission is something that you and your founding team are passionate about and can serve as your north star.
- Identify mentors who can help you refine key elements of the mission and concept of your solution.

Build

- Stay customer-obsessed as you build every feature, interface, integration, and security tool.
- Consult proxy customers and advisors at every major milestone, allowing them to help you refine your solution in a way that will make it more relevant, easy to use, and easy to purchase.

- Share your MVP or prototypes with these same stakeholders, further confirming the direction of your build.
- Identify interim products that may have value to your prospects, and sell them, or offer them for a reduced price, if possible.
- Consult with leaders (individuals or companies) that can assist you with regulatory compliance and security management.
- Find the right balance between frugality and extravagance to maximize dollars without stifling progress.

Launch

- Launch only when ready based on feedback from stakeholders; if they say it's not ready for primetime, rework the solution and ask again.
- Prepare your GTM carefully, as customers will not magically appear upon product launch.
- Have your security and data privacy approaches established to avoid any mishaps as you deploy.

Grow

- Work with partners and distributors to help accelerate growth and impact on the industry.
- Set up mechanisms for customer feedback like surveys and user groups (it's a great way to also conduct research for your product development roadmap).
- Ask for referrals as part of the customer feedback process.

There are many more lessons in this book, in addition to the ones mentioned above. Hopefully, you have found others that you can apply to your own journey. I began this book with, "No one starts a healthcare or life sciences company because they think it's easy." And that is still very true. But by reading this book, perhaps you have a deeper understanding of what it takes and are more prepared to become a market maker. Good luck!

11.9 Notes

____

____

____

____

____

Endnotes

1 The Startup Protocol, page 8.
2 https://www.federalregister.gov/documents/2024/12/04/2024-28361/marketing-submission-recommendations-for-a-predetermined-change-control-plan-for-artificial
3 https://techcrunch.com/2024/10/24/unitedhealth-change-healthcare-hacked-millions-health-records-ransomware/
4 https://jamanetwork.com/journals/jama-health-forum/fullarticle/2823757
5 https://hitrustalliance.net/about-us

Index

Note: Page numbers in *italics* indicate a figure, and page numbers in **bold** indicate a table on the corresponding page. Page numbers followed by "n" with numbers refer to notes.

B

C

D

E

F

G

H

M

N

O

P

R

U

V

W

X